WANT TO KNOW WHAT ARE THE OLDEST LIVING THINGS ON EARTH?

THIS IS WHERE YOU'LL FIND OUT!

THE OLDEST LIVING THINGS ON EARTH ARE THE MACROZAMIA TREES IN AUSTRALIA, BELIEVED TO BE BETWEEN 14,000 TO 15,000 YEARS OLD.

MODERN HISTORY'S OLDEST FATHER SIRED TWIN DAUGHTERS AT THE AGE OF 100.

THE YOUNGEST BALL PLAYER STARTED HIS CAREER IN THE BIG LEAGUES AT THE AGE OF 15 YEARS AND 10 MONTHS.

FACTS CAN BE FASCINATING. YOU'VE PROBABLY NEVER HEARD OF MOST OF THE FACTS COLLECTED HERE, BUT EVERY ONE OF THEM IS AUTHENTIC, ACCURATE, AND CAREFULLY CHECKED BY THE AUTHOR. YOU'LL LEARN THINGS YOU NEVER KNEW BEFORE . . . THAT THERE ARE MORE ODD FACTS ABOUT SCIENCE AND NATURE, MAN AND THE WORLD AROUND YOU, THAN YOU EVER IMAGINED. AND THEY'RE ALL IN THIS INTRIGUING *BOOK OF AMAZING FACTS*.

THE BOOK OF AMAZING FACTS

by JEROME S. MEYER

ILLUSTRATED BY

WILLIAM G. JOHNSON

PYRAMID BOOKS • NEW YORK

Dedicated to my good friend,
Peter Bodenheimer

THE BOOK OF AMAZING FACTS

A PYRAMID BOOK

Pyramid edition published June 1971

Printed in the United States of America

PYRAMID BOOKS are published by Pyramid Publications
A Division of The Walter Reade Organization, Inc.
444 Madison Avenue, New York, New York 10022, U.S.A.

CONTENTS

AMAZING FACTS

PREFACE

This is a book of superlatives, which, because they are so little known, become *amazing facts*. Here you will find the largest and smallest, the longest and shortest, the oldest and rarest, and many other extremes that become both interesting and informative. Here we see the world's largest flower, which measures 12 feet in circumference and 8 feet in height, contrasted with the world's smallest flower, which is between 1/30 and 1/50 of an inch in diameter.

You will also note that wood is the most useful substance to mankind, even more important than iron.

Here you will find man's greatest triumph as well as superlatives in scores of different categories.

In considering extremes of so many kinds the author has been continually conscious of limitations imposed by time. Every fact is true up to September 15, 1970; but that does not mean that all facts will be so forever. Surely there will be larger planes than the 747 and taller office buildings than the planned Sears Roebuck Company building in Chicago, and the same is true of numerous other items.

Some of the amazing facts are quite commonplace. Information about these may be easily obtained by looking through a *World Almanac*. These facts have been included because this is a book of superlatives and extremes and is intended not only to amuse and amaze but to instruct as well.

In collecting and assembling most of the facts in this book, some of the research was done through personal investigation and some through correspondence. In many cases back numbers of newspapers have provided full details of events at the time of their occurrence. In other cases considerable spade work and research was done digging through book after book in libraries of foreign consuls to get the correct material from foreign lands. In all cases, however, the information has been checked and rechecked for accuracy.

In addition to being a collection of unusual and fascinating facts of interest to both young and old, this book should have a considerable value as a reference book because of its uniqueness.

The author wishes to express his appreciation to William Johnson for the fine, clear illustrations that do so much to visualize and drive home a particular amazing fact. I also want to thank Meyer Goloboff for his valuable assistance in securing important data.

My everlasting thanks to Patricia Golbitz for her remarkable editing and valuable advice on bringing this book up to date.

J. S. M.

SCIENCE

Man's Greatest Triumph

ON JULY 20, 1969, AT 4:17 P.M. (E.D.T.), THE crew of the Apollo 11, after overcoming 88 separate steps and displaying incredible skill and courage, made a successful landing on the moon. This is by far the most amazing fact and man's greatest accomplishment.

The crew consisted of Neil A. Armstrong, Commander, Michael Collins, Commander Module Pilot, and Edwin D. Aldrin, Lunar Module Pilot. Through TV and radio hundreds of millions of people followed the activities and the clear transmission across 238,000 miles of space. This was another triumph and amazing fact.

Commander Armstrong, as he set foot on the surface of the moon, made the famous statement, "That's one small step for a man, one giant leap for mankind." And a jubilant President Nixon remarked: "This is the greatest feat in the history of the world since the creation. As a result of what you have done the world has never been closer together."

Wood: The World's Champion Material

IF YOU STOP TO THINK OF THE THOUSANDS OF different substances there are on the earth . . . some very valuable and some worthless, you may wonder why such a common thing as wood is the most important to civilization. It might be argued that iron and steel are far more important than wood because of the worldwide use of them in building, automobile construction, tools and cutlery and hundreds of other uses. Certainly the element silver, which is the basis of all photography and used exclusively in the making of mirrors, is a vitally important element and might be compared with iron and steel in its importance.

Of course there are many other elements and substances that your first judgment would believe are far more important to us than wood. So why is wood the champion?

As you travel through the country by rail you probably don't give a thought to the millions and millions of wooden railroad ties that support the rails. All railroads everywhere are dependent on these ties. Undoubtedly you may fail to appreciate the hundreds of thousands of wooden houses, barns and other structures you see from the train windows.

All this use of wood throughout the world is almost insignificant when compared to the inestimable value of its use in the making of paper, which is civilization itself. It is inconceivable what our modern world would be like if there were no such thing as paper! There is no need to elaborate on the overwhelming uses of paper in business houses, libraries, educational institutions and a great many more vital areas, not to mention the use of paper from wood pulp in the manufacture of cartons large and small for packaging and shipping, as well as of smaller boxes of all kinds.

Iron: The World's Most Important Metal

IRON IS BY FAR THE MOST IMPORTANT OF ALL METals and, as a matter of fact, it's a close runner-up to wood in usefulness.

So called "soft iron," when insulated copper wire is wound around and around it, forms perhaps the most important invention since the wheel thousands of years ago. No other invention in modern time can compete in value with this "soft iron" and copper wire combination otherwise known as

THE ELECTROMAGNET

Without the electromagnet practically every modern electrical instrument would be unknown. There could be no: telephone, television, telegraph, radio, electric bell, news ticker, traffic lights, movies, push-button elevators and other push-button electrical devices and no electric generators. They would not exist without a piece of "soft iron" with insulated copper wire wound around it, which runs our world.

The other vast importance of iron is that it is the

main constituent of steel, and steel is by all odds the champion of all metals even though it is not an element. There are scores of different kinds of steel used for hundreds of different purposes, from cutlery to automobile bodies and building construction.

Not a day goes by that you don't use steel in one form or another, from early morning to late at night, for steel is the leading industry in the United States.

The typewriter on which the manuscript of this book was typed consists of hundreds of small parts of steel. The linotype machine that set the type is also made of hundreds of steel parts. Indeed, the only time that steel did not play a major part in the production of this book was the molding of the type metal, which is made of antimony and lead. In the same way, every other manufactured product is dependent upon steel.

Every machine and machine part in the world is made mostly of steel. The skeleton of every tall building, every locomotive, ball and roller bearing, railroad rail, ocean liner, machine tool, tin can and article of cutlery is made from one or more metallic elements alloyed in various percentages with iron and called by the general name of steel.

The Great Hale Telescope

I HAVE CONSULTED AN ASTRONOMER AT THE Hayden Planetarium who told me that the Great Hale Telescope had not been moved and it is still the largest in the world.

The famous 200-inch Hale reflector telescope is at Mt. Palomar. It is 800,000 times as powerful as the human eye, which can see only a few thousand of the billions of stars in the heavens. By means of this giant instrument more than six thousand million stars can be seen and discerned; the frontiers of the universe are pushed back some thirty times, enabling man to peer into space a distance of more than 1,200,000,000 times the distance light, traveling at the rate of 186,000 miles per second, will travel in a year. This turns out to be 7,038,835,200,000,000,000,000 miles.

Of course the casting of the glass (pyrex) for the giant mirror was one of the greatest scientific triumphs. It required the very highest skill and precision on the part of everyone in the Corning Glass Works and took eleven months of constant watching and loving care to produce a perfect slab, free from any strains or imperfections due to improper cooling. The mirror was polished to an accuracy of one millionth of an inch of specifications, so imagine the responsibility taken by the polishers—the slightest error or slip would have ruined the entire job.

The completed mounting of the mirror in the tube was another great achievement which required the brains, experience and ingenuity of our best astronomers and engineers. The entire mounting weighs in the neighborhood of a million pounds and is so large that it includes a complete astronomical laboratory in itself. Perhaps the most amazing fact of all concerning this telescope is that, heavy and massive as it is (it's the equivalent of an eight-story building), it is so delicately balanced on its oil bearings that it may be moved by the mere touch of a finger.

The World's Longest-burning Lamp

THE WORLD'S LONGEST-BURNING ELECTRIC LAMP was made by the General Electric Company in Cleveland in 1949. It is a tiny neon glow-lamp which will burn steadily for three years. It is used on switchboards, radios and electrical apparatus to indicate whether the current is on or off.

The World's Smallest Electric Lamp

IN THE PICTURE THE MAN IS POINTING TO THE General Electric's "grain of wheat" bulb used in bronchoscopes and surgical devices. This tiny lamp consumes .17 watt and weighs about a 500th of an ounce. It is less than a tenth of an inch in diameter and slightly more than one third of an inch long.

Incandescent Lamp That Equals 100,000 Watts

ON JULY 27, 1949, AT THE RIVOLI THEATER IN New York, Twentieth Century-Fox installed and operated the world's largest electric light. The occasion was the premiere of the movie *Come to the Stable.*

This huge lamp was 35 inches high, had a bulb 20 inches in diameter and weighed 35 pounds. Although it was 50,000 watts it produced double the efficiency and was equivalent to 1,000 hundred-watt lights all concentrated into a single giant globe with power enough to run 250 washing machines or supply the lighting of 40 average country houses. The filament, which was as thick as a lead pencil and weighed 1.6 pounds, took enough tungsten to make 56,000 60-watt lamps. The intense heat of this light was enough to set a newspaper on fire at a distance of 6 feet and consequently it had to be shut off every ten seconds for cooling.

This enormous lamp was built by the General Electric Company in 1939 for exhibition at the New York World's Fair.

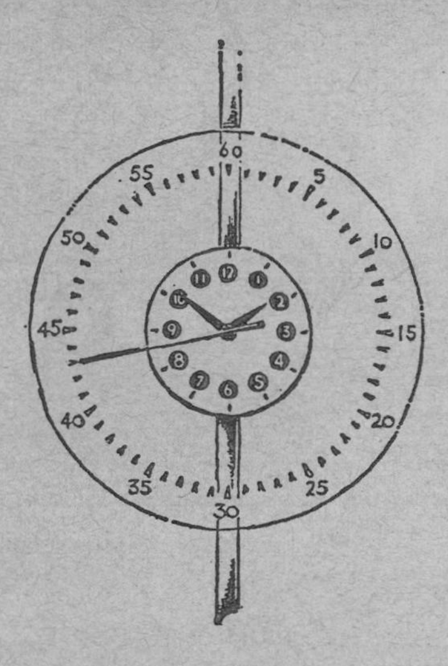

Time Accuracy to .05 of a Second

THE MOST ACCURATE PUBLIC CLOCK IN THE WORLD IS in the central window of the American Telephone and Telegraph Building on lower Broadway, New York. Designed by research physicists of the Bell Laboratories, it never varies from the official time (Naval Observatory time in Washington) by more than .05 second, which is about the time required for an express train traveling 60 miles per hour to go 4 feet. The secret of this remarkable accuracy lies in the special, exceptionally steady electric current which drives the hands. The current is controlled in the Bell Laboratories and is accurate to one part in ten million.

This clock is synchronized every 15 seconds with the Time Bureau of the New York Telephone Company, which gives the correct time to telephone users in the New York metropolitan district when they dial MEridian 7-1212.

A Source of Powerful Radio Energy

QUASARS ARE CELESTIAL OBJECTS, 4 TO 10 BILLION light-years away from earth. These small luminous bodies are sources of powerful radio energy; another name for them is *quasi-stellar radio sources.* Their existence was not established until November, 1962, but by March, 1967, more than 200 had been discovered. One quasar, 3C 446, is believed to be undergoing the most violent explosion detected, since it has increased 20 times in brightness in less than a year.

New Rocket Power

ION-POWERED ROCKETS WILL BE ABLE TO GO UP TO 100,000 mph. This is what the experts predict for craft in space that are fueled by electrically charged atoms. The first rocket in flight powered by an ion discharge was the Russians' Mars probe, *Zond II.* It was launched on November 30, 1964.

The World's Most Sensitive Balance

WILLIAM AINSWORTH & SONS, MANUFACTURERS OF analytical and assay balances for the United States Bureau of Standards, write the following about their Micro Balances:

We do not know of any more sensitive balances that are made commercially. It has been claimed that weighings of 0.0002 mgs. are made on some of them. Now one mg. (milligram) is equal to one thirty-thousandth of an ounce. Two ten-thousandths of a mg. is therefore equal to one one-hundred-and-fifty-millionth of an ounce. The ink required to make a single *i*-dot on this page weighs more than that!

It is almost impossible to conceive the weight of anything as light as .0002 mg., yet this remarkable balance can detect it.

The illustration shows this balance. The hood on top contains a filament lamp whose light is focused on a mirror fastened to the top of the knife-edge arm. This light is reflected to another mirror at the top of the hood and thence to a scale on the floor of the balance case. The very *slightest* movement of the arm is detected by the moving reflection on this scale.

The Smallest and Dumbest

IN THE *New York Times* OF MAY 19, 1950, A NEWS item announced that the world's smallest and dumbest mechanical brain had been invented by Edmund C. Berkeley, an electrical engineer at Columbia University in New York.

Christened "Simple Simon," this new electrical demonstrator of stupidity, which was only the size of a suitcase, could add 1 and 2 but could go no higher because its knowledge of numbers was limited to the digit 3. With all its 48 pounds of vacuum tubes and other electrical equipment it proudly blinked out the sum of 1 and 1 and even managed by the telegraph tape method to add 1 and 2 correctly, but when asked how much 2 and 2 are it stopped its noisy calculations and lit up its red distress signal light, which clearly indicated that it wanted help. The machine took five months to make and cost the inventor $540. Mr. Berkeley was not discouraged with Simon. He said he'd grow up and work on "real problems" some day.

One of the World's Most Amazing Machines

THE MULTIPLICATION PROBLEM THAT IS SHOWN ON page 24 would take the average person about fifteen minutes to do, plus another ten minutes to check for accuracy—and the chances are there would be many errors in the work, with a headache at the end for one who did the multiplying. As you can see, fourteen digits are multiplied by fourteen digits to get a twenty-eight-digit result. Not one person in a thousand could run this tremendous problem off accurately in less than fifteen minutes. If you think you can do it, try another pair of fourteen-digit numbers.

The Selective Sequence Electronic Calculator, made by the International Business Machines Corporation, can do the above problem in *one fiftieth of a second*—and it will be absolutely correct! It can multiply together fifty different pairs of fourteen-digit numbers similar to this one in one second. It can also divide 33 pairs of fourteen-digit numbers in one second and can add a nineteen-digit number to another nineteen-digit number in one 3500th of a second.

In a few minutes it can perform 9,000 multiplications, 10,000 additions and subtractions and more than 1,800 values from trigonometric tables. It solves the most intricate problems in the theory of numbers, the theory of the complex variable and plays with extremely difficult Gamma and Beta functions (in advanced calculus) the way you and I would play with a very simple problem in addition.

It has solved, in 103 hours, a series of differential equations in nuclear physics that would take a scientist 100 years to do with pencil and paper. Here is that equation relative to uranium fission:

$$U(z_i) = 2\rho_e^2 \int_{z_1}^{z_0} dz \frac{\rho(z)}{g(z)} \left\{ \left[\rho(z) + \rho(z_i) - \frac{d\rho(z)}{dz}(z - z_i) \right] K(k^2) - 2\rho(z_i) D(k^2) \right\}$$

The mathematics involved is long and tedious because it requires the solution of many differential equations in sequence.

IBM did not pretend that the machine would be a substitute for the human brain. It says the human brain is "here to stay" and nothing can equal it. The machine is merely a tool to save the scientist years of time that can be put to creative thought.

Since the Selective Sequence Electronic Calculator was in use the IBM computer has taken over. It is not described here because it's vastly complicated and requires a great deal of study and training to operate.

According to IBM it is more amazing than the Selective Sequence Electronic Calculator and hence has the honor of being the most remarkable machine for calculations in the world; but the Selective Sequence Calculator is still one of the great giants of computation.

```
              76428987314275
              83529674665193
              --------------
             229286961942825
            687860885828475
            76428987314275
          382144936571375
         458573923885650
        458573923885650
       305715949257100
      535002911199925
     458573923885650
    687860885828475
   152857974628550
  382144936571375
 229286961942825
611431898514200
----------------------------
6384088445351553654894530075
```

NATURE

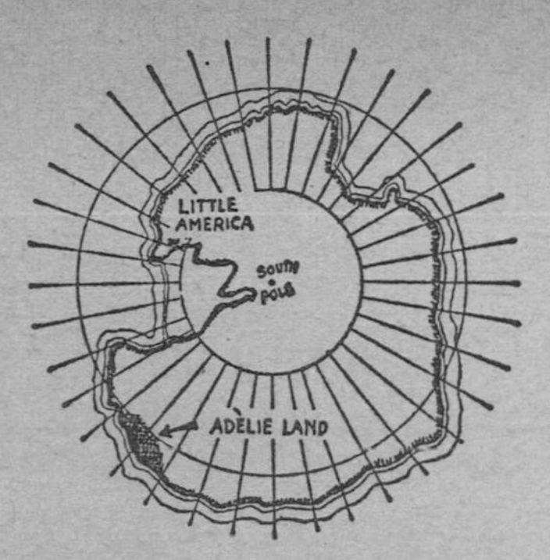

The Windiest Spot on Earth

IF YOU THINK THE CORNER OF STATE STREET AND Michigan Avenue in Chicago is windy just take a little trip to Adèlie Land at latitude between 66 and 67 degrees south, longitude between 136 and 142 degrees east. This land is the windiest spot on the face of the globe. According to Sir Douglas Mawson, the average wind velocity is 50 miles per hour, which, to us, would be a very severe gale. Prolonged hurricanes of 100 miles per hour or more are common in this region of Antarctica. To appreciate how windy this South Polar land really is, try to imagine a mild cyclone in your town every day of the week and a violent hurricane every Sunday, all year round.

The weather on Mount Washington, New Hampshire, in winter is also extremely severe. The highest wind velocity ever recorded in this country occurred there in 1934 and measured 231 miles per hour.

The World's Highest Tides

THE HIGHEST TIDES IN THE WORLD ARE IN THE BAY of Fundy, which separates New Brunswick from Nova Scotia. At the head of the bay, and at certain times of the year, the tides come in and go out at the astounding rate of 10 feet per hour, or 60 feet from highest to the lowest tide. This is about two thirds as fast as the water rises in the average bathtub with both faucets going full strength, and it keeps it up for six hours twice a day. If you stood on the mud in your bathing suit at the head of the Bay, the ocean water would be up to your knees in ten minutes' time and would be over your head in forty minutes. This rate of flow of 2 inches per minute causes a great deal of disturbance and renders the bay dangerous in certain places for navigation. The water is never still—either it is pouring into the bay or pouring out of it. Tides of 60 feet, however, are unusual and only occur in certain parts of the Bay at certain times of the year. The average rise and fall of the water is about 40 to 50 feet every six hours and this is quite enough to make the Bay of Fundy tides the greatest in the world.

The Driest Populated Spot on Earth

THE LITTLE TOWN OF ARICA ON THE CHILE-PERU border is the driest populated spot on the face of the earth. Situated in the very arid Chilean province of Tarapacá, the town's 14,000 people see an average yearly rainfall of only .02 inches, which is less than any desert region in the United States. This is all the more remarkable when one considers that Arica is facing the Pacific Ocean. Arizona is the driest state with an average annual rainfall of only 7.81 inches, so you can judge how dry the town of Arica is with only .02 inches.

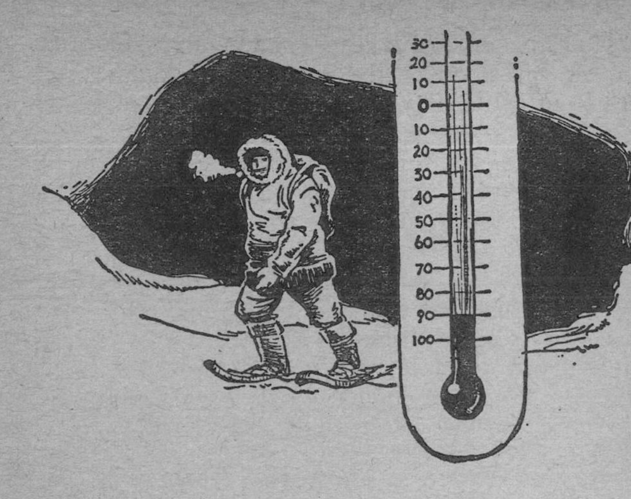

The World's Icebox

THE WORLD'S ICEBOX IS NOT THE NORTH POLE. IT IS in the Taiga country in north central and northeastern Siberia. This section, located 1,400 miles from the North Pole, is the coldest place on earth. The city of Verkhoyansk in eastern Siberia has the distinction of registering the lowest natural temperature ever recorded. This was 90 degrees below zero, Fahrenheit. At this temperature queer things happen. Over the years stone and silt have accumulated on ice, completely hiding the ice core, and we have a peculiar land formation whose central core is ice. If this part of the world should ever become warm for any length of time and the inside ice were to melt, islands would fall apart and "melt away." Of course at 95 degrees below zero ice is like stone and snow is like table salt. If there is the slightest breeze your breath will make little crackling sounds as it freezes and floats away. If you run and get out of breath at this low temperature the air is sure to coat your lungs with rime and cause you untold pain. If you stand still for five minutes without the proper clothing and protection you will be a stone corpse. At 90 below, rubber is as brittle as thin glass and mercury is as hard as steel.

Of course temperate-zone dwellers could not stand this terrible cold but it has certain advantages over our climate. It is almost impossible to catch cold or to get any other germ disease, because most germs cannot live in such extreme cold. Food, of course, can be kept for years and years without spoiling, a fact that was proved by the Byrd expeditions.

The reason for this climate is very high mountain range on the south of the Taiga country. Warm winds from the south are cut off while the intense cold from the Arctic regions sweeps down on the unprotected side. The city of Verkhoyansk is in the center of all this and it gets more than its share. A remarkable and almost incredible fact is that this Russian city is hot in the very short summer it has and the thermometer often reaches 80 degrees above zero. This makes Verkhoyansk the city of greatest extremes in temperature in the world, ranging from 80 above to 80 below in a typical year.

Freak Weather Records

IN THE 24 HOURS BETWEEN JULY 14 AND JULY 15, 1911, at Baguio on the Island of Luzon in the Philippines, 46 inches of rain fell. If an empty tank had been placed out of doors when the rain began, it would have had nearly 4 feet of water in it only twenty-four hours later! On each acre of ground in Baguio 5,400 tons or 1,350,000 gallons of water fell from the sky in that twenty-four-hour period. This is the world's record for a day's rainfall.

The record for a short shower goes to Portobelo, Panama, on May 1, 1908, when 2.47 inches of rain fell in 3 minutes.

During the winter of 1906 and 1907 in Tamarack, California, 884 inches of snow fell. This is a little more than 73 feet of snow, and if it had fallen in a single blizzard it would have completely buried the entire city and every building in it. Seventy-three feet of snow in one season is the world's record fall anywhere.

Hot Stuff

THE HIGHEST NATURAL TEMPERATURE EVER RE-corded sent the thermometers in Azizia (about 25 miles south of the city of Tripoli in North Africa) in Libya up to 136 degrees in the shade on September 13, 1922.

According to the United States Weather Bureau, the heat in the sun in the summer is usually 30 to 40 degrees higher than it is in the shade; and in Africa, where a great deal of radiation from desert sands takes place, the temperature difference is much greater. Assuming the sun's temperature in Azizia on September 13, 1922, to be 180 degrees (a conservative estimate), a pail of cold water left out in the sun for an hour would become scalding, though it would not boil. Eggs dropped into this water would poach. The sand and sidewalks would be far too hot to touch without very severe burns and, of course, walking out in the sun without a hat or umbrella would be almost sure suicide.

An unofficial report to the Weather Bureau stated that on July 6, 1949, a freak heat wave, lasting just two minutes, sent the thermometers on the central coast of Portugal up to 158 degrees Fahrenheit—a world's record. As this lasted only two minutes and was not confirmed it must be taken for what it is worth.

The Most Dangerous Animal

IN SELECTING THE WORLD'S MOST DANGEROUS ANImal we naturally have a wide choice. A bull when excited is extremely dangerous. A man-eating tiger is certainly not a house pet and neither is a king cobra. It all depends upon what we mean by dangerous.

By dangerous we mean a beast that is enormously powerful and, at the same time, always mean and aggressive. A bull will not harm you unless you annoy him; a tiger will not bother you unless he is particularly hungry. But there is one beast that stands out above all others for power, fierceness and aggressiveness. He is the black buffalo of South Africa.

The black buffalo is found all the way from the Cape of Good Hope to the Congo and is known as the "Cape" buffalo. He is one of the most powerful animals alive with enormous muscles, massive head and horns as strong as steel. He is always mean and fierce. He will charge at almost anything that is alive, and the only way to escape certain death is to get out of his path as quickly as possible. More hunters have been killed by this ferocious beast than by any other anywhere in the world.

The Smallest Bird in the World

THE TINY FAIRY HUMMINGBIRD OF CUBA IS THE smallest known bird in the world. It is hardly ever more than 2¼ inches long and weighs less than 1/200 of an ounce. Its nest is only ¾ of an inch in diameter and the eggs, which are seldom more than ¼ of an inch long, hatch little birds which are smaller than many insects.

One of the most amazing facts in this book is the complexity of this tiny organism with its four-chambered heart, complete digestive, reproductive, respiratory, nervous and muscular systems inside of a skeleton, and all coming out of an egg ¼-inch long.

The fairy hummingbird of Cuba has been referred to as a "flying gem" and Audubon called it "the glittering fragments of the rainbow" because of its brilliant plumage of dazzling red or green or yellow or almost any other color. The wings of this bird move so fast they produce a blur and a soft humming sound. Its feet are small and delicate and hardly ever used. In spite of all its beauty and its tiny size it is tough and absolutely fearless. It will fight birds four and five times its size and frequently win out.

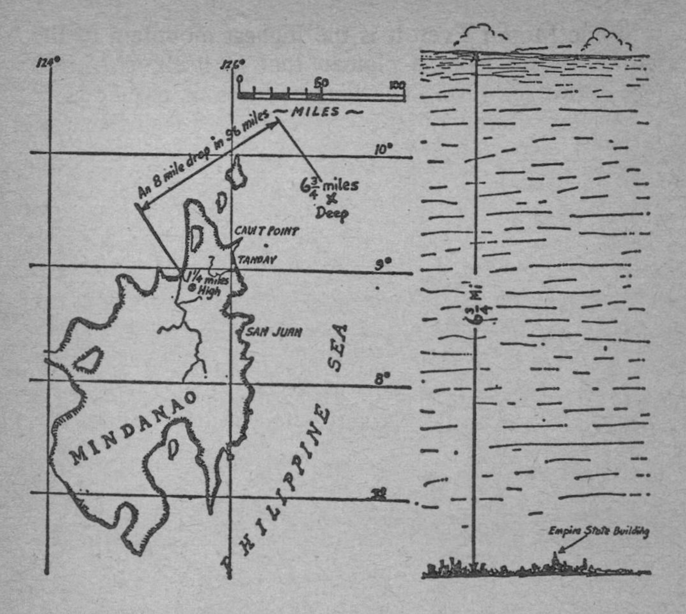

A Vertical Drop of More Than 12 Miles

THE DEEPEST PART OF THE WORLD IS LOCATED 50 miles northeast of Cauit Point on the island of Mindanao, the southernmost island in the Philippines. Here the ocean floor is 35,400 feet or 6.75 miles below the surface. The drawing, which was done to the scale of ¾ inch = 1 mile, shows how high above New York City and the Empire State Building the surface of the water would be. The map gives the location of the Mindanao Deep (shown by the X) and also shows an 8-mile drop in the short distance of 96 miles.

Of course everyone knows that the highest point of the earth is the tip of Mount Everest in southern Tibet. This is 29,141 feet above sea level. Now 29,141 feet is 5½ miles, and if this is added to the 6.75 miles of the Mindanao Deep we get a total of 12.25 miles between the highest and the lowest points on the earth's surface. If you could fall that distance it would take you 63 seconds; you would be traveling nearly 25 miles per minute before you hit the ocean floor.

While Mount Everest is the highest mountain in the world it rises from a plateau that in itself is 15,000 feet above sea level. The highest mass of mountain in the world is Mount McKinley, which has a single precipice drop of 14,500 feet—the highest in the world.

The World's Longest-lived Animal

THERE IS QUITE A CONTRAST BETWEEN THE LONGest-lived plant and the longest-lived animal. The Macrozamia trees in Australia (p. 00) live to be more than 10,000 years old but animal life is much shorter. Of all the animal life on earth the giant tortoise of the Galapagos Islands is said to be the longest-lived. Some of these reptiles have been known to live two centuries—and 200 years for any form of animal life is a very long time. The giant tortoise used to be extremely plentiful but the species is now becoming extinct. The average tortoise weighs more than 600 pounds and has a shell 4 feet in length.

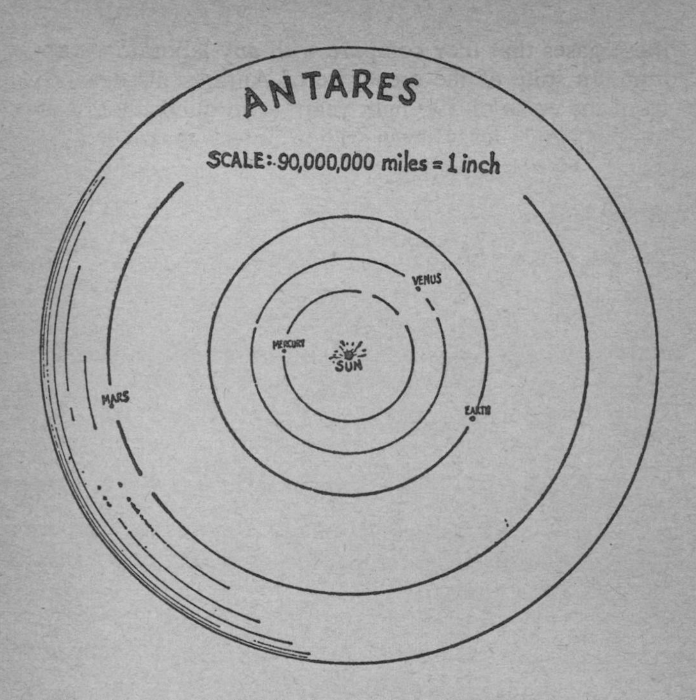

The Largest Thing in Existence

WHAT IS THE LARGEST THING IN EXISTENCE?

To try to answer this apparently simple question we must be willing to accept the definition of "thing" as a "portion of matter" remembering that matter is not always visible or touchable. Air is matter and so is any gas or mixture of gases.

As far as we know at present the giant star Antares in the constellation Scorpio is the largest or certainly one of the largest things in existence. It is more than 110,000,000 times the size of the sun and approximately 125,000,000,000,000 times the size of our tiny earth. To appreciate the enormity of this star, examine the diagram, which is drawn to a scale of 90,000,000 miles to the inch. It shows the center of Antares in the center of the sun and the outside surface far beyond the orbit of Mars.

Antares is made up of the rarest gases. So thin are

these gases that they compare with any laboratory vacuum. In spite of the great size of Antares, its distance from the earth of 390 light years (two quadrillion, two hundred and eighty-seven trillion miles) makes it difficult to see without a telescope.

The Longest Flying Bird in the World

THE ARCTIC TERN, A SEA BIRD BELONGING TO THE gull family, flies an average of more than 22,000 miles every year, which is more than most traveling salesmen do. This remarkable bird is always on the go flying from the Arctic to the Antarctic regions and back again year after year. It flies low over the water preying on small fish and other sea life and enjoying the midnight sun in summer in the Arctic and in winter in the Antarctic. The amazing energy and wanderlust of these birds has baffled naturalists, for there is no other animal in existence that travels such enormous distances under its own power.

The Largest Flying Bird

No satisfactory explanation has ever been given for the amazing power which seems to be stored up in the wings of the albatross. This bird can sail through the air for an hour at a time without the slightest visible motion of its expanded wings.

Found mostly in the southern oceans—the South Pacific and the South Atlantic, the albatross is the largest flying bird, the full-grown albatross having a wingspread of about 12 feet from tip to tip. The wing is not more than 9 inches wide so it resembles a very narrow strip rather than a wing. The enormous spread of this bird is gained by elongation of the inner bones of the wing and by increasing the number of small secondaries. The body of the bird weighs about 18 pounds and is about 4 feet long.

How Swift Is the Swift?

THE FASTEST BIRD IN THE WORLD HAS BEEN APPROPRIATELY called the swift. Its body resembles a torpedo in shape and its wings are very long and narrow. The American cloud swift has been known to fly circles around an airplane traveling at the rate of 85 miles per hour. This amazing bird can attain speeds anywhere from 170 to 200 miles per hour and its cousin in India or Australia, known as the Indian swift or Australian spine swift, can reach a speed of 250 miles per hour. This seems to be the upper limit of speed for animal life. But this dizzy pace is slow indeed when compared with the speed of the Cephenomyia fly, which holds the record for any form of life anywhere in the world.

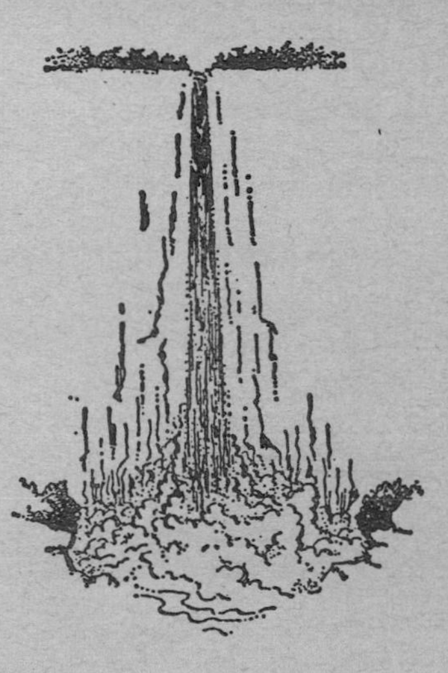

The Highest Waterfall—Nearly a Mile High

IN THE JUNGLE WILDS OF VENEZUELA IS A PLATEAU which, in the words of Jimmy Angel, is "about 9,000 feet high and a quarter to a half a thousand square miles in extent." Through this plateau runs the Caroni River, which at one point plunges over the cliffs to form the world's indisputably highest waterfall.

Jimmy Angel, an American soldier of fortune, discovered this waterfall in 1937 while flying over the jungle, and today it bears his name.

Angel Falls is twenty times as high as Niagara and more than a thousand feet higher than any other known falls on earth. Conservative estimates put the height at 3,300 feet, while some who have seen the falls say it appears to be about a mile in height. Its nearest competitor is the Kukenaäm, also located in Venezuela, which is only 2,000 feet high. Just to keep the record straight, here are the ten major waterfalls of the world —and the height is always in one, unbroken leap:

1.	Angel Falls, Venezuela	3,300 feet
2.	Kukenaäm, Venezuela	2,000 feet
3.	Sutherland Falls, New Zealand	1,920 feet
4.	Tugela, South Africa	1,800 feet
5.	Yosemite, California	1,750 feet
6.	Ribbon Falls, California	1,600 feet
7.	King George, British Guiana	1,600 feet
8.	Krimmler Falls, Austria	1,490 feet
9.	Roraima, Venezuela	1,480 feet
10.	Gavarnie, Pyrenees in France	1,390 feet

The King of Poison

THE DISTINCTION OF BEING THE MOST POISONOUS living thing in the world goes to the king cobra of Siam. Not only are its glands larger than those of any other animal or insect but its fangs can deliver more deadly venom. In most cases the bite of the king cobra proves fatal within three hours and in many cases death occurs in less than one hour. The venom of the cobra dissolves and paralyzes the nerve cells, seriously damages the blood cells and acts on the respiratory system, causing slow suffocation while the heart becomes overstimulated. With the exception of the Cape buffalo of Africa or the Indian buffalo of India, the king cobra of the jungles of Siam is the most dangerous animal in the world.

Quite an Explosion

ON AUGUST 27, 1883, THE VOLCANIC ISLAND OF KRAkatoa, between Java and Sumatra in the South Pacific, exploded, sending millions of tons of dust twenty miles into the air, destroying more than 300 villages and killing about 36,000 natives. The noise of the explosion was heard on the island of Rodriquez 3,000 miles away, and the great air waves resulting from the explosion circled the entire earth seven times, affecting barometers everywhere. Dust from this island settled in every part of the world for weeks afterward. The island of 18 square miles, which rose from 300 to 1,400 feet above the sea, was blown to pieces and in its place there was a submarine cavity 1,000 feet below the sea. This was unquestionably the greatest explosion and loudest noise in the history of civilization. The illustration shows the explosion compared with that of an atom bomb.

The Heaviest Thing in Existence

BY "HEAVY" WE REALLY MEAN "DENSITY," WHICH is the amount of matter packed into a given volume. Iron is heavier than wood because it has greater density than wood. The heaviest metal on the earth is the element-metal osmium. A baseball made out of osmium would weigh more than forty regular baseballs.

Now one of the densest things in existence (according to present knowledge) is the white dwarf star called "The Companion Star of Sirius." Sirius is a brilliant star in the constellation Canis Major and may be seen any winter night in the United States. This dwarf star is very near Sirius. It is 61,000 times as dense as water.

So dense is this star that if the star dust from it were substituted for salt in your salt shaker, not only would your table collapse from its weight but the floor would probably collapse also. One cubic inch of this star weighs a ton so that an ordinary suitcase filled with it would weigh as much as 8 large locomotives. A wedding ring made from this star material would weigh as much as a baby elephant and would certainly be difficult to place on the finger of a bride.

Of course there may be other unknown stars that are denser than the "Companion to Sirius." Ven Maanen's Star is, according to theory, "several million times as dense as water" but the actual verification of this has not yet been established.

Too Big for a Corsage

THE LARGEST FLOWER IN THE WORLD BLOOMED IN the New York Botanical Gardens on June 8, 1937. It is the *Amorphophallus titanum,* or giant calla lily. The drawing shown here is taken from a photograph made on that date in Bronx Park, New York. The flower itself is 8½ feet tall, 4 feet in diameter and 12 feet in circumference. It was the largest specimen ever seen in cultivation. Its native home is Sumatra.

Strictly speaking, this giant is not really a flower but an inflorescent, as the botanists call it. Inside the lower base there are hundreds of tiny flowers, but they are hidden from view and the observer sees only the enormous outer plant. Flower or not, this colossal plant is the largest single type of calla lily ever to be seen, and deserves to hold a world's record for interest as well as size. Unfortunately, this inflorescent has an unpleasant odor resembling decaying meat.

All botanists agree that the largest single flower is the *Rafflesia arnoldi* when it is in full bloom. It is a tropical flower related to the buttercup, but it has degenerated to such a degree that its roots, stem and leaves are not formed at all. The seeds germinate and become a fungus, like a huge stemless toadstool. In full bloom the flower is from 3 to 6 feet in diameter with a very unpleasant odor.

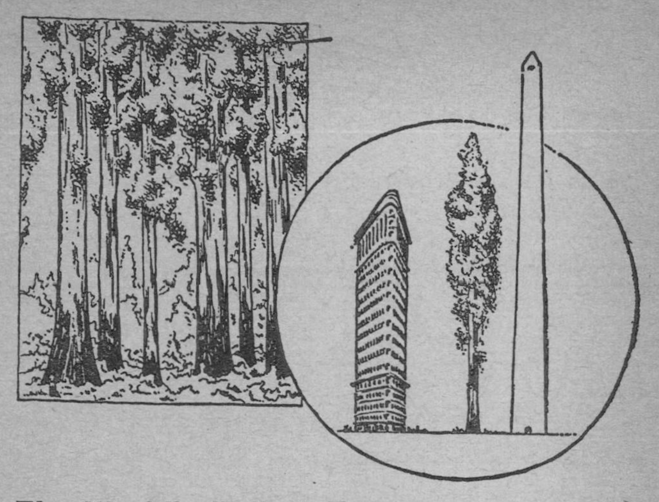

The World's Tallest Tree

OF THE HUNDREDS OF BILLIONS OF TREES ON THIS earth there must be one tree that is taller than any other. The question is: where is that tree?

The tallest trees in the world are located in California and Australia. The redwoods of California rise to the dizzy heights of 300 feet or more and, according to J. Barton Herschler, custodian for the Muir Woods National Museum, the tallest tree on earth is 364 feet high. It is a redwood, located a few hundred feet east of Dyerville Bridge on the Redwood Highway in California. It is known as the "Founders Tree."

In Australia, in the mountains of Victoria, New South Wales, and in Tasmania, there are forests of enormous eucalyptus trees (known as *Eucalyptus amygdalina* or peppermint gum trees) that rival the California redwoods. Bushmen's claims of having measured giant trees over 500 feet in height have never been officially verified, but there is a huge *Eucalyptus regnans* that rises to a verified height of 362 feet. This is 2 feet less than the great Founders Tree in California.

In an article entitled "Nature's Skyscrapers" by Thomas Dunbabin, an Australian journalist, we read that a British Admiralty Pilot, "an unassailable authority on these matters," measured a tree on Ceram Island in the Moluccas, Netherlands East Indies, which is 428 feet tall. This tree has apparently been checked by British Navy surveyors and is undoubtedly the tallest tree yet found on the earth. This is equivalent to the height of a 35-story building and is 64 feet higher than the Founders Tree.

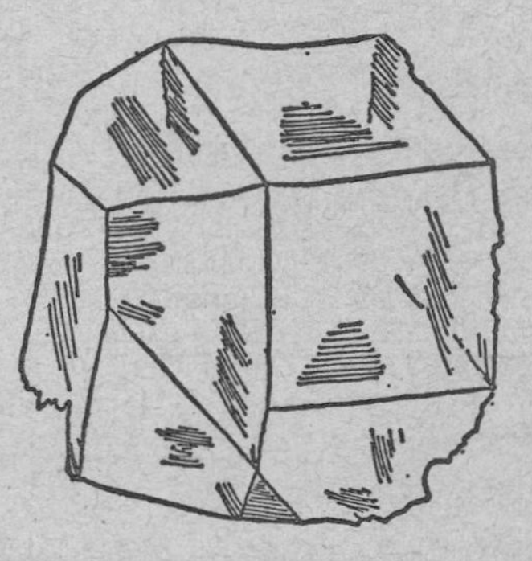

The Largest Gem

THE LARGEST GEM IN THE WORLD IS IN A GLASS CASE in the American Museum of Natural History in New York City. It is a huge topaz taken from the Minas Geraes in Brazil and it weighs 596 pounds or 1,380,000 carats. It is not particularly remarkable to look at and most visitors to the museum pass it by for more thrilling gems in other cases.

The Greatest Earthquake

ON THE MORNING OF NOVEMBER 1, 1755, THREE quakes shook Lisbon. The first occurred at 9:40 A.M. and lasted about one minute. It was a mild series of tremors too weak to cause alarm. After a respite of half a minute there came a series of rapid shocks so violent that houses everywhere started tumbling to the ground. This lasted two minutes and completely destroyed the greater part of the city. After a pause of a minute the earth movement changed and everything was violently shaken up and down as you might shake a cocktail shaker—this lasted for three long minutes, completing the ruination of the entire city and flattening nearly everything in it.

No true estimate of the dead was given because the bodies were carted off in carloads without any attempt to count or identify them. Accounts vary from 30,000 to 60,000 dead in the city of Lisbon alone and many more in the remote sections of Portugal. Out of 20,000 houses less than 3,000 remained standing, and there were no traces of streets, lanes, public places or anything else. Everything was reduced to small mountains of rubble. Soon after the 9:40 quake fires broke out and completely destroyed what little the quake had spared. Many of the survivors fled to the Cays Depreda, a strongly built quay near the Lisbon Custom House. At the second great shock which came at 10 A.M. the nearby river rose 20 feet and quickly subsided. Instantly the entire quay sank with all the people on it and boats and small craft were sucked in like water going down a drain. No trace of quay or any of the people was ever found.

The repercussions of this terrible quake were felt over an area of 1,400,000 square miles, covering Portugal, Spain and most of southern France. The water in thousands of lakes, rivers, canals and pools within this vast area started to oscillate violently like water in a pail that is suddenly jerked up and down. Windows were smashed in Bordeaux 610 miles away, and the tremors were felt as far north as Scotland.

A third great shock occurred at noon, nearly two and one-half hours after the first shock. As soon as this died out the ocean rose in giant waves 50 and 60 feet high. So violent were these waves that they traveled all the way to the British coast two hours later, causing damage to some towns on the Channel.

This was undoubtedly the most severe earthquake in history, even though it may not have caused the greatest number of deaths. The center of the quake was computed to be about North Latitude 39 degrees and West Longitude 11 degrees.

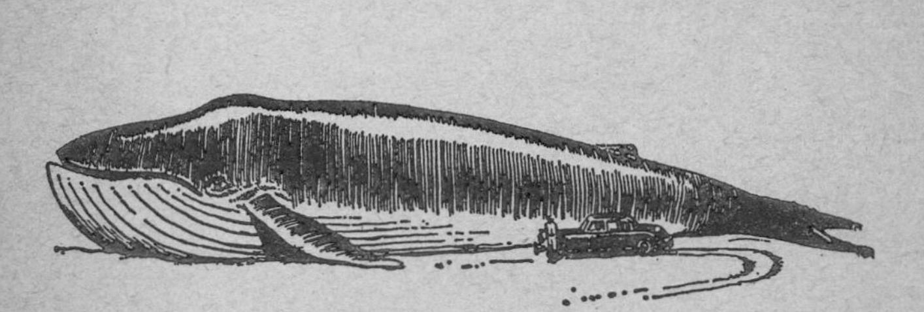

The Largest and Most Powerful Animal in the World

THE WHALE IS THE LARGEST AND MOST POWERFUL animal that ever lived on this earth at any time. It is as much larger than a man as the man is larger than a newborn kitten. One of the largest whales ever caught weighed nearly 120 tons and measured 116 feet long and 20 feet across. If this creature could stand up vertically it would be as tall as the average lighthouse.

Whales are capable of amazing feats of strength. An instance is on record where an Antarctic killer whale, in an attempt to attack some sleigh dogs stranded on an ice floe, dived deeply under the floe and swam very swiftly upward with such force that the ice, which was nearly 5 feet thick, was splintered into tiny fragments.

Another instance of whale power concerns Captain Nelson's whaling expedition off the Siberian coast when the Captain's boat made fast to a giant blue whale. Although the engines of the boat were pushing it full speed in one direction, the whale succeeded in pulling the boat in the opposite direction for seven hours at a speed never less than 8 knots (about 10 miles per hour). What other living creature could show such remarkable power?

The Fastest Four-legged Animal

THE WORLD'S SPEEDIEST FOUR-LEGGED ANIMAL IS not, as many people might think, the greyhound or the gazelle. It is the cheetah. Over short distances there is no animal in the world that can even approach it for speed. Though the cheetah has been timed at 103 feet per second, or 70 miles per hour, it can do better than that. The black buck, which is the fastest of Indian antelopes, is supposed to be unbeatable, but you can give this fleet-footed animal a 200-yard head start over a cheetah and the cheetah will bring him down before they have run a quarter mile. Many authorities say that the cheetah can race along at 80 miles per hour, which is about as fast as the fastest crack train on the New York Central or Pennsylvania Railroads.

The cheetah, sometimes called the hunting leopard, is found throughout Africa and southern Asia and has been used for centuries in India for chasing the black buck or Indian antelope and other fast game.

The Winning High and Broad Jump

THE WORLD'S RECORD BROAD JUMP AND HIGH JUMP belongs to the gazelle, which can cover the ground in hops 12 feet high and 40 feet long.

The Largest and Smallest in Seeds

THE LARGEST SEEDS IN NATURE ARE THOSE FROM the palm tree which, to botanists, is the *Lodoicea seychellarum*. The seeds are huge and often weigh as much as 30 pounds. They resemble double coconuts and, when planted, produce trees that grow to heights of 100 feet or more. In contrast to these large coconut seeds, the almost unlimited number of microscopic seeds inside a single seed capsule of an orchid appear quite small. So small are these orchid seeds that more than seventy million of them fit neatly inside an average seed capsule. Being so small they are disseminated readily by the wind, but few of them produce orchids.

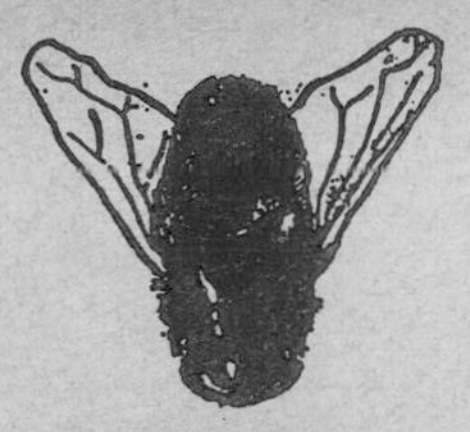

Speed Champion of the World

NO LIVING CREATURE ON EARTH CAN BEGIN TO COMPETE with the little deer botfly, otherwise known as the Cephenomyia, for speed. No vehicle or propeller-driven airplane can come anywhere near approaching the enormous velocity of this insect.

The Cephenomyia, according to Dr. Townsend, has been clocked at 818 miles per hour, or a little more than 13 miles per minute. The wonderful efficiency of its wing base and the tremendous power stored up in its muscular system are partly responsible for its speed. It flies so fast that it appears as a blurred streak, no sooner detected than out of sight. The flight time was checked over and over again with the shutter of a high-speed camera and the data thus obtained are as accurate as possible. To quote directly from Dr. Charles Townsend, a noted scientist who devoted many years to the study and behavior of this type of insect:

> Regarding the speeds of Cephenomyia, the idea of a fly overtaking a bullet is a painful mental pill to swallow, as a friend has quaintly written me, yet these flies can probably do that to an old-fashioned musket ball. They could probably have kept up with the shells that the German Big-Bertha shot into Paris during the World War. The males are faster than the females, since they must overtake the latter for coition. Then the males habitually fly at higher altitudes than the gravid females, and thus encounter less friction which enables them to attain greater speeds. Besides the gravid females are heavily laden with ova and young, which must make them slower than the males. At 7000-foot levels in the Sierra Madre val-

leys of western Chihuahua I have seen the gravid females pass while on search for hosts at a velocity of well over 300 yards per second—allowing a slight perception of color and form but only a blurred glimpse. On the other hand, on 12,000-foot summits in New Mexico I have seen pass me at an incredible velocity what were quite certainly the males of Cephenomyia. I could barely distinguish that something had passed—only a brownish blur in the air of about the right size for these flies and without sense of form. As closely as I can estimate, their speed must have approximated 400 yards per second." (From the *Journal of the New York Entomological Society*, Vol. XXXV.)

While it is true that physicists have disputed Dr. Townsend, claiming that it is impossible to time an insect so small whizzing through the air at that terrific speed, they admit that the Cephenomyia *does* travel exceedingly fast. The fact that it appears to be nothing more than a blurred streak is evidence of its enormous speed and it is safe to say it is the fastest thing alive—even if it moved at only 500 miles per hour.

The Smallest Flowering Plant

THE TINY GREEN COATING ON FRESH-WATER PONDS consists of millions of separate flowering plants which vary from one-thirtieth to one-fiftieth of an inch in diameter. This is Wolffia and Wolffiella, otherwise known as duckweed. The stem hangs down into the water and a root cap is formed at the base of it. The duckweed is considered the smallest flowering plant known and is about one seventy-millionth the size of the giant *Amorphophallus titanum*. A comparison of this with the largest flower known indicates the vast range in the size of flowers.

The Biggest Rainfall

CERTAINLY THE WETTEST PLACE ON EARTH IS CHERrapunji, India. Here the average annual rainfall is 427 inches or 35 feet. This means that on every square foot of ground more than 270 gallons of water fall each year —and this is just the *average;* some years it is more than that. In the single month of August, 1841, 20 feet of water poured down on this Indian town. This is the world's record rainfall for any month anywhere.

The Highest Wave

THE HIGHEST OFFICIALLY RECORDED OCEAN WAVE occurred near Manila in the Philippines on the night of February 6, 1933. The wave was computed to be 112 feet from trough to crest. This is about the height of a ten-story building.

The Largest Living Thing in the World

IT IS NOT AN EASY MATTER TO SELECT THE LARGEST living thing in the world. We know that the largest animal is the whale and we also know that the giant Sequoias in California are larger than any animal. Of course these gigantic trees might well be considered the largest living things in the world.

But it all depends upon the definition of "large." For our choice we name the *Gaylussacia brachycera,* which in English means the wild box-huckleberry of eastern Pennsylvania. This plant, though only a foot or so above the ground, covers as much as two or three acres of ground. A single plant that covers that much ground is certainly the largest plant in the world. It is sterile to pollen and has practically no seeds at all. It thrives on humus derived from dead oak leaves, and its main part grows underground.

In addition to being the largest known plant, it is considered by many authorities to be the oldest living thing on earth and is often called "the plant of the past —the Methuselah of huckleberries." Some estimates place its age at 11,000 years but that is indefinite. Whether it is older than the Macrozamia trees of Australia is anyone's guess.

Nothing Is Lazier Than the Sloth

THE LAZIEST LIVING ANIMAL IN THE WORLD IS THE tropical American sloth, which hangs for weeks and months from the branches of trees without moving perceptibly. It feeds on the leaves of the tree and is nearly always upside down. The sloth is a nocturnal, silent mammal living most of its uneventful life alone. It does manage to reproduce, but the female can have only one offspring.

The Oldest Living Thing in the World

THE OLDEST LIVING THING ON THE FACE OF THE earth is said to be the Macrozamia tree of the Tambourine Mountains in Queensland, Australia. Naturalists and other scientists have estimated these trees to be between 12,000 and 15,000 years old, but there is no positive proof that they are actually as old as that.

The Macrozamia tree is somewhat like a palm. Each year a new ring of scales appears on the outside of the trunk, as shown, and as the tree grows, these scales are pushed down toward the bottom of the trunk. As they move down they become smaller and smaller until they are mere scratches that finally fade out entirely into the massive woody pulp of the trunk. For this reason it is almost impossible to determine the exact age of the tree, since counting of these outside scale-like rings is impossible. It is much easier to determine the age of the huge sequoias of the West or even the giant bald cypress tree in the little Red Indian village of Santa Maria Del Tule, which is claimed to be more than 4,000 years old.

Referring to a particular Macrozamia tree in Queensland, Dr. William Malisoff of the University of Queensland says in his book *The Span of Life:* ". . . The Great Grandfather Peter at an age of approximately 15,000 years was cut down by vandals in 1937 and, after three months, started to grow again upon replanting. It is now in three sections assembled in place by some 200 workers. So slow-living is this giant that 10 or 12 years must elapse after being cut down before its complete death."

There is some difference of opinion with regard to the actual age of the Macrozamia trees but it is safe to say they are the oldest living things on earth. The giant bald cypress of Mexico that measures 185 feet around the trunk and is definitely known to be more than 4,000 years old is younger than many of the Macrozamias in the Australian mountains. These trees were old when Moses was a boy and they will be living when our great-great-great grandchildren have great-great-great grandchildren.

PEOPLE

The First Woman In Space

VALENTINA VLADIMIROVNA TERESHKOVA IS THE FIRST woman to orbit the earth. On June 16, 1963, Junior Lieutenant Tereshkova was launched in Vostok VI from Baikonur, U.S.S.R., at 9:30 A.M. Her flight lasted 2 days, 22 hours and 46 minutes. She traveled 1,225,000 miles, completing 48 orbits around the earth, landing on June 19 at 8:16 A.M. She is married to cosmonaut Andreyan Grigoryevich Nikolayev. Their child is the world's first child born of space-traveling parents.

The Oldest New Father

THE REVEREND JAMES E. SMITH OF CARBONDALE, Illinois, was 101 on March 16, 1950. Just sixteen months before his 101st birthday he became the father of twin girls, thereby baffling medical science. His wife was sixty-four years younger than he, which, incidentally, is another kind of record. They were married in 1935. Smith's mother-in-law was almost young enough to be his granddaughter. Besides the twins, the Smiths had four sons. It is a rare occasion when a father is eighty-eight years older than his oldest son and nearly a hundred years older than his youngest daughter.

Very Heavy Going—710 Pounds

ROBERT, A FARM BOY FROM ILLINOIS, HAD A RARE pituitary gland disorder that ran wild and boosted his weight to 375 pounds by the time he was ten.

Robert had to quit school in the sixth grade because he could not walk any distance, and he kept on gaining until at the age of twenty he weighed 710 pounds. He spent most of his time sitting on a specially reinforced stool, reading pulp magazines.

Robert's chest measurement was 102 inches; his knees, 33 inches around. His overalls required nine yards of material and his shirts five. He ate normally and slept seven hours a night, but dozed off in the daytime. When he retired for the night he had to go through the doors of his home sideways and his two normal brothers had to lift each leg into bed. He bore his burden very well and his cheerfulness and good humor made him a favorite with everyone who knew him.

150,000 Totally Useless Words

THE LONGEST SPEECH ON RECORD WAS MADE BY United States Senator Huey Long, who, after 15½ hours of constant talking, dropped into his seat from physical exhaustion.

The speech was a filibuster, aimed against the NRA. It began at 12:30 P.M. on June 12, 1935, and lasted until 4 A.M. of June 13. It used up about 150,000 totally useless words, which, in addition to political fireworks, included many irrelevant quotations, cooking recipes and dozens of humorless jokes. It filled 100 extra pages in the next morning's *Congressional Record,* costing the Government $5,000.

The Greatest Linguist Who Ever Lived

CARDINAL JOSEPH CASPAR MEZZOFANTI, ONE OF THE most remarkable men in history, was born in Bologna on September 17, 1774.

At an early age he learned the carpenter's trade, and it was while he was working at his bench that he heard an old priest giving Latin and Greek lessons to a number of students next door. As he worked at his bench Mezzofanti absorbed every word of these lessons and soon was able to converse fluently in both languages, though he had never seen a Latin or Greek book.

When he was an obscure priest, Mezzofanti was called in one day to confess two men who were condemned to die the next day. Not able to understand their language the priest went home and, that night, learned it so well that he not only was able to confess the criminals but was able to converse fluently with them.

Here are thirty-nine languages that Cardinal Mezzofanti spoke *as fluently as anyone speaks his native tongue:*

1. Albanese
2. Algonquin
3. Amarinna
4. Arabic
5. Armenian (ancient)
6. Armenian (modern)
7. Basque
8. Bohemian
9. Californian
10. Chaldee
11. Chinese
12. Coptic
13. Danish
14. Dutch
15. English
16. Flemish
17. French
18. Geez
19. German
20. Greek
21. Guzarati
22. Hebrew
23. Hebrew (rabbinical)
24. Hindustani
25. Illyrian
26. Italian
27. Latin
28. Magyar
29. Maltese
30. Persian
31. Polish
32. Portuguese
33. Romaic
34. Russian
35. Spanish
36. Swedish
37. Syriac
38. Turkish
39. Walachian

In addition to these thirty-nine languages the Cardinal spoke (not fluently) the following:

1. Angolese
2. Bulgarian
3. Chilean
4. Georgian
5. Gypsy languages
6. Koordish
7. Mexican
8. Pegu
9. Peruvian
10. Serbian
11. Welsh

Mezzofanti understood the following languages though he did not speak them as fluently as he spoke the thirty-nine first mentioned:

1. Burmese
2. Bimbarra
3. Chippewa Indian
4. Cochin-Chinese
5. Singhalese
6. Cornish
7. Delaware
8. Frisian
9. Gaelic
10. Irish
11. Icelandic
12. Japanese
13. Lappish
14. Lettish
15. Oceanian
16. Malay
17. Quechua
18. Sanskrit
19. Tibetan
20. Tonquinese

And incidentally, Cardinal Mezzofanti understood thoroughly thirty-seven other dialects not mentioned above.

He Needed Half a Dozen Tombstones

ACCORDING TO THE RECORDS, Chief Lepodotemachoselachogaleokranioleipsanodrimupotrimmatosiphioparaomelitokatakeclummenokichleipkossuphophattoperisteralektruonoptegkephalokigklopelsiolagoosiraioealetraganopterugon died in Wisconsin in 1866.

The record does not say what this Indian's *first* name was nor does it indicate what he was called for short (probably Lepodotemachoselachogaleokraniol). Neither is there any record of how many envelopes were necessary to address a single letter to him. But it is certain that no other name in the entire history of the human race can match this 178-letter giant for length.

The Shortest Name Is Zero

IN FEBRUARY, 1950, AT THE LITTLE TOWN OF Neuilly-Plaisance in France, M. and Mme. O celebrated their golden wedding anniversary. That was all to their surname—just the letter O. Since the abbreviation for Monsieur is simply M., you can see how much ink was saved in writing to this gentleman. His name on the envelope was "M. O"; the shortest surname of any person anywhere.

Sir 754

DIWAN BAHADUR SIR TIRUVALYANGUDI VIJAYARAghavacharya claimed to have the longest name in the world and we doubt if anyone disputed him. He was a short and affable Indian gentleman who arrived in America on September 1, 1949. When reporters asked him his name he treated them to five seconds of what sounded like pure Indian. Not understanding the one-sided conversation they asked for his name again and he responded with "I just told it to you." In order to keep the record straight he wrote his name on the blackboard as shown, and this satisfied everyone. Of course few people called the Diwan by his real name. He said his friends called him "Diwan," which means prime minister; his children whittled his name down to "pop" and ladies called him "Dear One." In London the Diwan was called "Sir 754" because that was the number of his room at the Savoy Hotel.

The Most Prolific Inventor of Modern Times

THOMAS EDISON, THE WIZARD OF MENLO PARK, PATented 1,150 inventions and did more for modern progress than any other human being. Edison's early boyhood is known to most of us. He was very poor in school work and, in his own words, he was "always at the bottom of my class." Born in Milan, Ohio, on February 11, 1847, he spent his boyhood in Port Huron, Michigan. His mother, a highly educated woman and schoolteacher by profession, was his main source of information and inspiration although she was not always gentle with him. She gave him a sound thrashing after he had induced a boy employed by the family to swallow a large quantity of Seidlitz powders to see if the gas generated by them would enable the boy to fly. But she always encouraged him in his insatiable thirst for scientific knowledge and, while the family was not poor or needy, she permitted him to take a job selling newspapers on the trains of the Grand Trunk Railway between Port Huron and Detroit so he could earn his own money and build his own chemical laboratory in the cellar of their home.

Edison went from one job to another because his active mind was always "thinking up new ideas" and he seldom paid attention to his work. At twenty-two he drifted into the New York offices of the Law Gold Reporting Company and, seeing the very crude ticker tape machine out of order, suggested how to repair it and improve its efficiency. He promptly got a job with the company at $300 a month, and it was at this time that he started inventing the stock ticker.

The amazing list of Edison's better known inventions follows:

1871. Assisted Sholes, the inventor of the typewriter, to make the first successful working model.

1872–76. Invented the monograph, the automatic telegraph systems, duplex, quadruplex, sextuplex and multiplex telegraphic systems. Invented paraffin paper.

1876–77. Because of his deafness and his inability to hear the crude Bell instrument he invented the carbon telephone transmitter, which not only made the telephone commercially practical but paved the way for the modern microphone.

1877. Invented the phonograph, which he improved in 1878.

1879. Invented the electric light. The first incandescent bulb lit on October 21, 1879.

1879–80. Invented sockets and switches and many improvements on dynamos. Invented the magnetic ore separator.

1883. Discovered the principle of the radio vacuum tube known as the "Edison effect" and later developed into the vacuum tube that makes radio possible.

1887–90. Took out about 400 patents on improvements of his earlier inventions, many of them on improvements of the phonograph.

1891. Perfected the motion picture camera and paved the way for the modern moving picture industry. Took out a great many patents on electric railroad signals.

1892–1900. Patented a great many important inventions relating to the crushing of huge rocks.

1900–1910. Invented improvements on storage batteries and Portland cement.

1905. Invented the dictating machine.

Thomas Alva Edison died on October 18, 1931, and the entire world mourned his death. The *New York Times* gave 4½ full pages to him and his lifework and he was called the greatest benefactor of humanity in modern times.

BUILDINGS

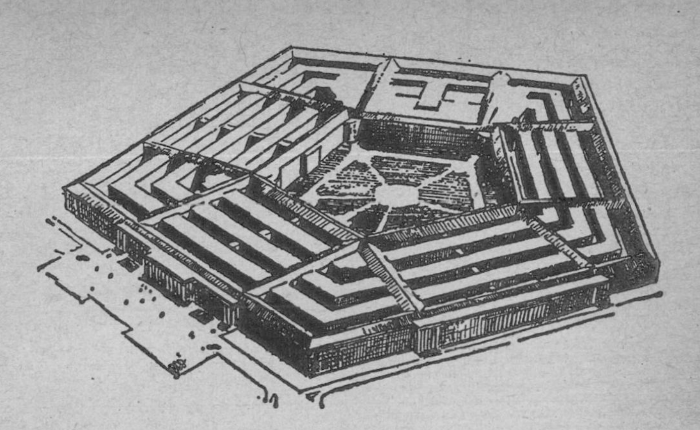

The World's Largest Office Building

IF YOU THINK THE 102-STORY EMPIRE STATE BUILDing or the 73-story RCA building in New York is the largest in the world you are wrong. Many people think the great Merchandise Mart in Chicago holds the record, but it doesn't. The honor goes to a 5-story structure in Washington known as The Pentagon.

So enormous is this building that it would take you nearly fifteen minutes to walk around it only once and if you started at 9 A.M. and walked, without once stopping, through every one of its inner corridors, you would still be walking at 1 P.M. By the time you had completed the tour of the entire building you would have walked more than 17 miles! Each side of the Pentagon measures 926 feet so it is impractical to photograph it from the ground since it won't fit on one plate. The best way to show this huge building is from the air.

The Pentagon consists of five long inner rings of buildings connected by ten corridors. Its total floor area of 6,000,000 square feet adds up to 150 acres or nearly a quarter of a square mile. During the war the Pentagon housed 38,000 workers daily—enough to equal the population of Quincy, Illinois, or Elkhart, Indiana. The private telephone exchange in this building contains 68,000 miles of trunk lines.

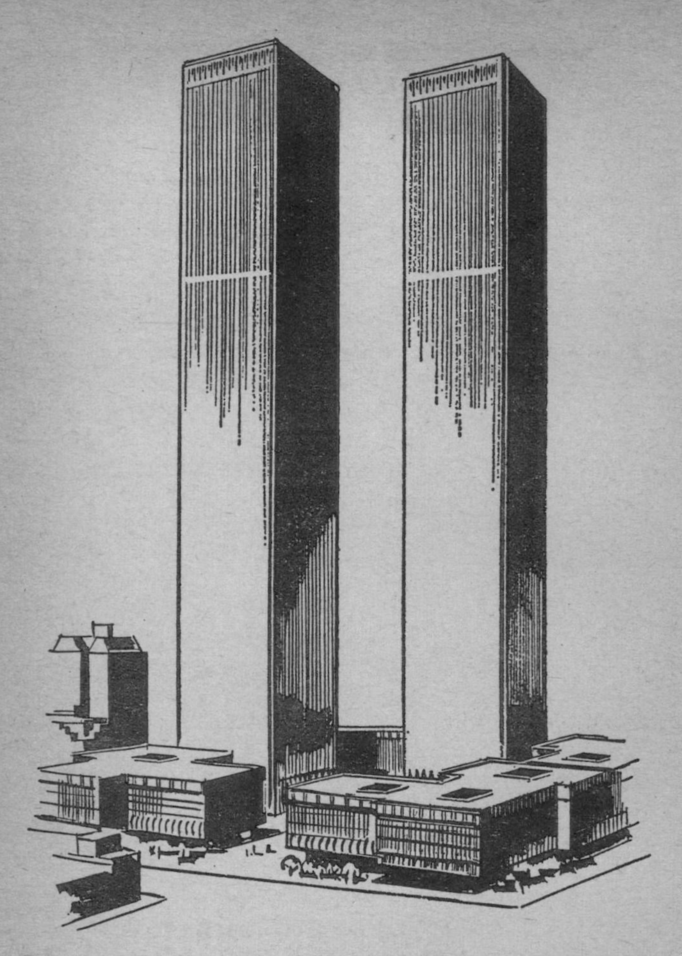

The World's Tallest Building

FOR MORE THAN FORTY YEARS THE EMPIRE STATE Building in New York was the world's tallest. It is 102 stories rising 1,250 feet above Fifth Avenue. Now it has to acknowledge that the two enormous towers of the World Trade Center in lower Manhattan are taller. When completed they will rise 110 stories or 1,350 feet above a five-ace park-like open plaza, as shown here.

These two buildings will have 9,000,000 square feet of usable space and are a building project like no other in size, complexity, and revolutionary concept. However, the length of time these two gigantic buildings will hold a record will be short. The Sears Roebuck Company in Chicago will erect its new headquarters building soaring 1,450 feet into the air, which will be finished in 1974. This will be 100 feet higher than the World Trade Center, which will be completed in 1971. As a New Yorker recently quipped, "The Trade Center will be the world's tallest building for the world's shortest time."

The World's Largest Hotel

THE LARGEST HOTEL IN THE WORLD IS LOCATED IN Moscow. It is the Hotel Rossiya. It contains 3,200 rooms providing accommodations for 6,000 guests in three separate buildings. The largest hotel in a single building, however, is the Conrad Hilton, which was formerly the Hotel Stevens, on Michigan Avenue in Chicago. It contains 2,600 guest rooms and rises 25 floors. It employs more than 2,000 people of whom more than 70 are telephone operators and 72 are elevator operators. These employees also include a medical department and a private fire department.

The Largest Church

ST. PETER'S IN VATICAN CITY STATE IS THE LARGEST church in the world. This great structure, one of the finest pieces of architecture in the world, took two centuries to build. The general design of the building is credited to the architect Bramante, but it was considerably altered by the great artist and architect Michelangelo. He designed the magnificent dome and painted the ceiling of the Sistine Chapel—a colossal job that took the master two years to accomplish. While this was in progress Raphael decorated the papal apartments. The painting *The Last Judgment* by Michelangelo, which took him six years to complete, together with all the other works has made St. Peter's one of the storehouses of the world's finest art.

It takes about 50,000 people to crowd this great church and more than 80,000 have attended services there at one time. The length of St. Peter's is 1,151 feet—a little more than one fifth of a mile—and its width is 767 feet. It contains 8 grand staircases, 20 large courts and 11,000 rooms of various sizes. The great avenues of pillars and colonnades are roofed by 162 enormous statues.

The Smallest Church

THE TINY CHURCH OF MONTE CASSINO, ACCOMMODATING only three worshippers, stands on a hill overlooking Latonia on the outskirts of Covington, Kentucky.

The inside of the church is very plain. The walls are 8 feet high with an arched ceiling. There are three rough prayer benches facing a tiny altar. The interior of the stone belfrey is so small it cannot accommodate a bell and the church from the outside resembles a mausoleum.

This church was built in 1850 by the Benedictine Fathers and few travelers have ever visited it. It was named after Italy's famed monastery, Monte Cassino, the cradle of the Benedictines, which was bombed to ruins in World War II. In spite of its midget size this church has a long and interesting history.

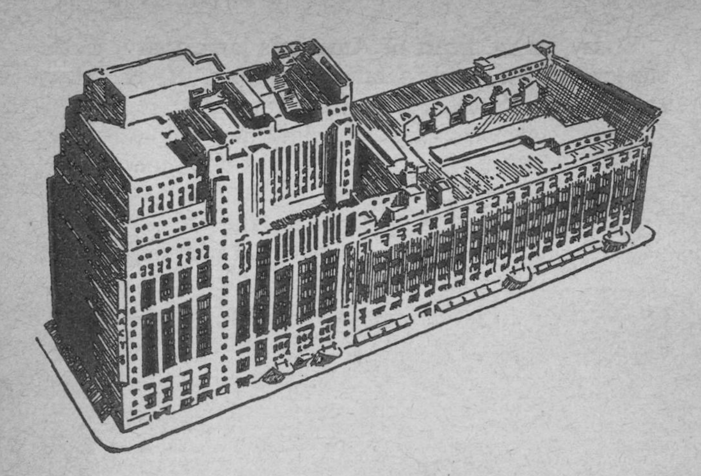

The World's Largest Department Store

On October 28, 1858, near Fourteenth Street in New York, an unpretentious little fancy dry-goods shop opened at 204 Sixth Avenue. In this small store, the owner, Rowland Hussey Macy, displayed on three long counters linens, gloves, laces, ribbons, embroideries, feathers, artificial flowers and hosiery.

During the first year the Macy business was so good that he had to hire fifteen sales people to take care of the customers. At the end of that first year he had spent all of $2,800 in advertising and his total business amounted to nearly $90,000.

In 1860 the little dry-goods shop became a full-fledged department store with separate departments completely stocked with china, glassware, luggage, sporting goods, etc., and by 1874 the Macy business occupied the ground floor space of eleven different stores. In that year L. Straus & Sons, a wholesale crockery house, agreed to stock two departments in Macy's and share the profits from those two departments. This turned out to be so successful that Straus and Macy became partners in 1888. In 1896 Straus & Sons acquired the complete ownership of the business and they retained the name of R. H. Macy & Company, Inc.

Today, in the heart of America's largest city, in the shadow of the world's tallest building, R. H. Macy stands as the world's largest department store.

Macy's occupies a square block in Herald Square. Only half of 2,012,000 square feet of floor space, however, is devoted to selling—the rest is given over to the service and operating divisions to take care of its employees. These include a roof lounge, a recreation room, a cafeteria, a hospital, a dental office, a library, a private bank, a testing laboratory, an advertising department, and a law library.

The Congressional Library

THE LIBRARY OF CONGRESS IN WASHINGTON, D.C., IS now the largest library in the world, outranking the British Museum and the famous Bibliothèque Nationale in Paris. It was established by an act of Congress in 1800 and, until 1897, it was housed in the Capitol. In that year it was moved to its present location directly east of the Capitol in a $7,000,000 structure which is the largest, most ornate and most costly library building in the world.

The Library of Congress occupies nearly four acres of ground and contains more than thirteen acres of floor space. In 1949 this enormous library contained 8,689,639 books, nearly two million maps and views, two million pieces of music and 300,000 phonograph records (the largest music library in the world),

175,000 rare books and hundreds of thousands of priceless original letters and documents. On the second floor, safely locked in an airtight case and watched constantly by an armed guard, are the original Declaration of Independence and Constitution of the United States. Among the rare books is one of the three existing perfect vellum copies of the Gutenberg Bible.

The United States Copyright Office is part of the Congressional Library and receives more than 350,000 books, pamphlets and prints yearly.

The World's Largest Indoor Theater

THE RADIO CITY MUSIC HALL IN NEW YORK, IN ADdition to being the largest indoor theater in the world, has a number of other superlatives to its credit.

The Music Hall seats 6,200 people and every week in the year more than 160,000 are entertained there. The auditorium is a city block long and nearly a city block wide. If you sit in the last row in the orchestra, the stage is so far away that the performers look like little puppets, yet the slightest sound on the stage can be heard all over this immense house.

The 144-foot-wide stage—the largest in the world—is big enough to accommodate three-fourths of a city block of 5-story buildings. The huge semicircular arch framing this stage is 120 feet in diameter and is closed by the world's largest curtain. This curtain contains more than 2,000 yards of fireproofing material and almost a mile of steel cable. Its enormous weight of three tons made it impractical to transport it in one piece, so it had to be carried to the Music Hall in five separate pieces and stitched together on the stage by a corps of sewing women.

The moving picture screen is also the largest in the world. It is 70 feet long and 40 feet high and was designed especially for the Music Hall. This gigantic screen could completely hide from view almost any country or suburban home. The entire screen is perforated to permit the battery of amplifiers directly behind it to transmit sound to the vast audience.

The Music Hall has fourteen projecting machines, four in the main projection booth, four in the preview rooms, two on the stage for scenic effects and four slide effect machines in the main projection room.

Enough electricity is used by the Music Hall in one year to supply the needs of a town of 7,500 population for the same period. The 25,000 light bulbs in the theater range in size from 2 watts to 5,000 watts. The 2-watt bulbs are used for program lights on the backs of the seats and the 5,000-watt bulbs are used for stage lighting.

The Radio City Music Hall has been called the "Showplace of the Nation." It was opened in December, 1932.

The World's Largest Bus Terminal

LOCATED IN THE HEART OF THE WORLD'S BUSIEST urban area, just a short distance from Times Square in New York City, the Port Authority's $24,000,000 bus terminal, the largest in the world, opened on December 15, 1950. Occupying the square block from Eighth to Ninth avenues and from 40th to 41st streets this giant terminal handles more than 130,000 passenger movements daily. The design of the structure provides for two bus loadings and unloadings. The lower level is for long-distance bus travel and the upper level for suburban and commuter's travel. The roof of the terminal is a parking lot for 450 automobiles fully equipped with ramps and escalators connected with the main concourse. A considerable portion of the 8 acres of floor space in this terminal is occupied by stores and restaurants.

The Largest Bank

THE LARGEST COMMERCIAL BANK IN THE WORLD IS The Bank of America in California. It was founded by Amedos Peter Giannine, who died on June 3, 1949, at the age of seventy-nine.

On December 31, 1969, the assets and total resources of the world's two largest banks were: Bank of America $25,573,116,000 and First National City Bank $23,091, 894,000.

Mr. Giannine was born in San José, California, on May 6, 1870. He entered the banking business when his father-in-law made him a director in a building loan association. In 1904, after a disagreement with his associates, he left the Columbus Building and Loan Association and started the Bank of Italy in San Francisco on a capital of only $150,000, contributed by a number of friends.

On April 18, 1906, the great earthquake of San Francisco occurred and Giannine fled through the streets with $2,000,000 hidden under a mass of vegetables in a pushcart. In 1907 the Bank of Italy was able to pay all its depositors in gold, which is one of the reasons why the bank began to grow.

In 1929 Giannine entered the New York banking field after having bought up a number of small banks. He purchased the Bank of America and consolidated it with his other purchases.

By the close of 1948 the Bank of America had 517 branches in California as well as branches in Tokyo, Manila, London, Kobe and Yokohama and had representatives in New York, Milan, Paris, Zurich and Shanghai. Its total assets at that time were $6,072,913,000 and it was then, as it is now, the world's largest bank.

The Largest Bell

THE WORLD'S LARGEST BELL STANDS IN A SQUARE IN Moscow. It was cast in 1733 and weighs 440,000 pounds. It is 19 feet 3 inches high and 22 feet 8 inches in diameter at the base. The tongue is 14 feet long and 6 inches in circumference.

This giant bell, formerly known as the Tsar Bell, was never in use. It fell down when attempts were made to hang it, and a piece broke from it. The Tsar set it up in a public square to be used for a small church, as shown. The broken piece is placed in front of the entrance.

TRANSPORTATION

The Largest Yacht

THE LARGEST AND MOST LUXURIOUS YACHT IN THE world belongs to the fabulous shipping magnate Aristotle Socrates Onassis. She is 325 feet long, was remodeled at a cost of $3,000,000 and christened *Christina.* She carries a crew of 46 with 25 bedrooms for guests and on a small portion of her deck there is a sailboat, a 5-seater sea plane, several life boats and an Italian automobile. The large game room contains two El Greco's, one over a mantel of Lapis Lazuli mosaic. And, yes, there is a large swimming pool with a mosaic tile bottom that is adjustable.

Elizabeth the Queen

WHEN THE FIRST QUEEN ELIZABETH OF THE CUNARD Line was launched it was the largest and fastest steamer in the world. A second Queen Elizabeth was built many years later and launched in 1969. It is 963 feet long with a tonnage of 65,863, and is known now as the fastest steamer in the world.

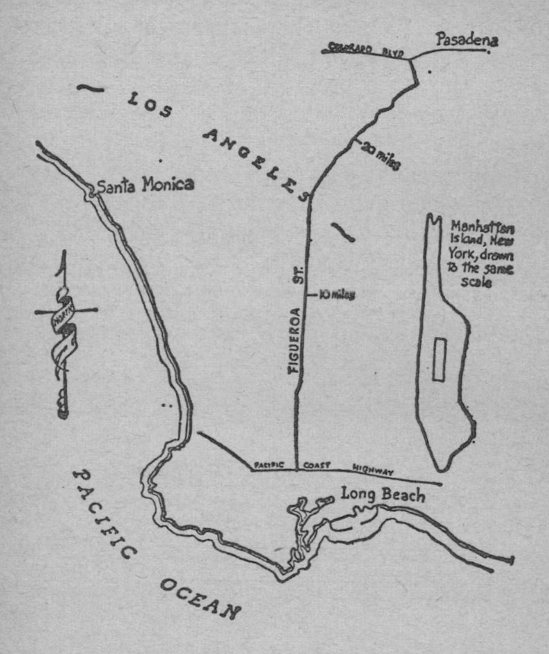

The Longest Street in the World

THE LONGEST STREET IN THE WORLD IS LOCATED IN Los Angeles. It is known as Figueroa Street and was named after the Mexican governor José Figueroa. It runs north and south through the city for a distance of 30 miles. It connects Pasadena in the north to San Pedro in the south and is the only street in the world that runs 30 miles through the same city. Broadway in New York City runs from the Battery to the Yonkers line, which is a little more than 16 miles and, while it continues to keep the name of Broadway, it runs through many cities and towns all the way to Albany.

The World's Widest Street

THE WORLD'S WIDEST STREET IS THE MONUMENTAL Axis, running from the Municipal Plaza to the Three Towers Plaza in Brazilia. The street is nearly 275 yards wide and runs for a mile and a half.

The World's Longest Suspension Bridge

FOR YEARS THE GREAT BRIDGE SPANNING THE Golden Gate from San Francisco to Marin County, California, was the longest suspension bridge in the world, but that is no longer the case. The distinction is now held by the Verrazano-Narrows Bridge, which spans the entrance to New York harbor, stretching from Staten Island to Brooklyn. The bridge cost more than $305,000,000 and was completed on November 21, 1964. It measures 6,690 feet between supports and carries two decks each with six lanes of traffic. The center span is 4,260 feet long; and the traffic in the first twelve months was 17,000,000 vehicles. The bridge was designed by Othmar H. Ammann, a Swiss-born engineer.

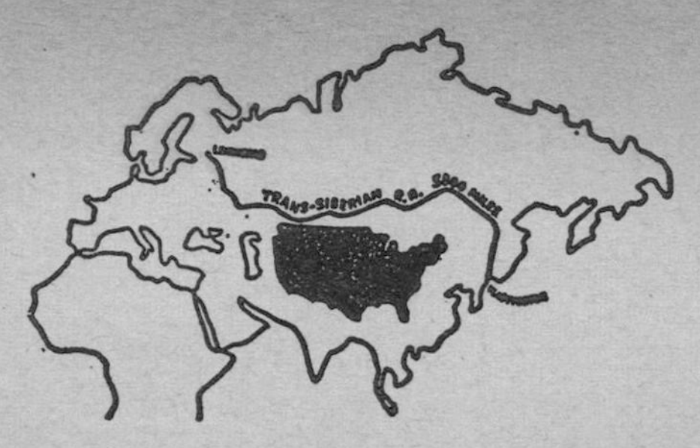

5,800 Miles of Continuous Railroad

THE WORLD'S LONGEST CONTINUOUS RAILROAD RUNS from Leningrad to Vladivostok, a total distance of 5,800 milcs, which is equivalent to the distance from New York to Los Angeles and back. It is the Trans-Siberian Railroad, binding European Russia to the Far East and, needless to say, it played a vital role in World War II. Trains leave Vladivostok every Monday, Wednesday and Friday for Leningrad and, in the twelve days and nights required to make this run, there are some 250 station stops. It's a long run, twelve days and nights on a train, and the Russians don't care too much for the trip, although most of them never do the entire route. The vast area covered by this two-track road is sparsely settled and the scenery becomes extremely boring. The desert waste land of central Siberia, however, covers some of the richest untapped gold and coal deposits in the world. Some day, perhaps, this land will be worth millions of dollars.

In 1946 a typical Trans-Siberian train consisted of a locomotive, 10 old-fashioned passenger cars, a "restaurant," a mail car, a sleeping car, four cars without bedding called "hard" cars, two regular cars with bedding called "soft" cars and a special car for mothers with small children. All these cars were crowded to capacity and the speed of the train seldom exceeded 45 miles per hour.

Subsequently the Soviet Union improved its railway system and added a few new locomotives. One of these was the powerful JS, or Joseph Stalin, which weighed 82 tons and could attain a speed of 81 miles per hour.

Pint-sized Railroad

ALONG THE ENGLISH CHANNEL'S CURVING COAST from Hythe to Dungeness and overlooking the Strait of Dover, runs the tiny Romey, Hythe and Dymchurch Railway, reputed to be the smallest public railroad in the world. The tracks of this road are only 15 inches wide, a little more than a quarter the width of the standard railroad track. On these tracks tiny steam locomotives, one quarter the size of the regular engines, travel on regular schedules—and the trains are never late on their 14-mile run. The passenger cars are about 15 feet long and can accommodate eighteen passengers each. Small as this road is it did its bit to help England stave off Hitler's promised invasion during World War II. It hauled tons of pipe for "Pluto," the famous undersea oil line to France which was so necessary to the Allied invasion of Europe. It also carried hundreds of AA batteries and troops and was always on the job for anything that might come up during the Battle of Britain. It is still running today and boasts a speed of 30 miles per hour, which is quite speedy for its size. It is privately owned and very efficiently run.

The World's Longest Tunnel

THE SIMPLON PASS BETWEEN SWITZERLAND AND Northern Italy was started on February 24, 1905. A double railway underpass was run through the Swiss mountains for a distance of 12.25 miles, and most of the work was done by 1912. World War I held up the completion of this remarkable tunnel until 1922. Boring and blasting this tunnel more than twelve miles long through a series of huge mountains took a long time and cost more than 65,000,000 Swiss francs ($16,000,000). The tunnel has two electrified tracks accommodating heavy locomotives of the Federal Railways all the way from Vallorbe to Domodossola.

Keep This Record Straight

THE LONGEST STRETCH OF STRAIGHT RAILROAD track in the world runs across the Nullarbor Desert in Australia. This track goes for 328 miles without once curving or crossing a river. During the entire train ride one cannot see a tree anywhere. It is undoubtedly the world's most boring trip.

The World's Largest Airport

IN ESTIMATING THE SIZE OF AIRPORTS THROUGHOUT the world two important things must be considered: first, the number of planes that come and go in a day, and, second, the actual area of the airport itself.

The busiest airport in the world is in Chicago. It is the Chicago International Airport: O'Hare Field. It had a total number of passengers in 1969 of more than 27 million and a total of more than 628,000 air-carrier movements in a year; or about a takeoff and landing every 45 seconds.

The largest airport in actual area is the Dulles International Airport in Washington, D.C., with an area of 9,880 acres, or nearly 16 square miles. This, too, is an extremely busy airport but not equal to the hustle and bustle of O'Hare Field in Chicago.

An airport now under construction will be located between Miami and Naples in Florida. When completed it will cover an area of approximately 39 square miles.

The airport that handles the largest volume of international flights is the John F. Kennedy Airport on Long Island, formerly known as Idlewild. It occupies 4,900 acres of land, equivalent to all of Manhattan Island south of Forty-second Street. Each of the runways is 200 feet wide and from 6,000 to 9,500 feet long. Stated in another way, this means that each runway is a city block wide, and from 1.14 miles to nearly two miles long. The runways accommodate more than 1,000 plane movements per day.

The John F. Kennedy International Airport is a city within a city, with office buildings, churches, a huge ultra-modern hotel, restaurants, theaters and shops.

The Largest Commercial Airplane

THE WORLD'S LARGEST COMMERCIAL AIRPLANE IS the Pan American 747. It has a cruising speed of 625 miles per hour and carries 362 passengers. It is 231 feet long with a wing span of more than 195 feet. The height of the tail above the ground is 63 feet and its fuel capacity is more than 47,000 gallons. The cargo and baggage space on this giant plane is 6,190 cubic feet and its payload 124,000 pounds.

LITERATURE

He Averaged 4 Books a Year for 30 Years

THE MOST PROLIFIC AMERICAN AUTHOR WAS Horatio Alger, who wrote, and had published, 119 full-length novels in thirty years. Besides this he was the author of hundreds of articles and poems that ran in the magazines of his time.

Alger was born in Revere, Massachusetts, on January 13, 1834. He was a graduate of Harvard in the class of 1852 and became a teacher and journalist in 1864. In 1868 he started writing books for and about boys, and by the time of his death in 1899, he had completed nearly 120 novels, averaging 4 books a year for thirty years.

Alger was nearly always the hero of his books. They were usually about poor-but-honest New York boys and their struggles to get ahead against heavy odds. They were, with few exceptions, hard-working, upright, teen-age youngsters who *always* became rich and famous. The books filled a great demand in an age of Elsie Dinsmore and the British Victorian period.

No list of juveniles today refers to Alger. Teachers have refused to admit his works to school libraries, claiming his style to be dull and unimaginative and his texts loaded with preachments. But Alger had an enormous influence on the youth of his day. He was by far the most popular writer, and everywhere, from small villages to large cities, his name was known. His books were sought after and read from cover to cover.

Alger's life ambition was to become a great novelist but, according to Herbert R. Mayes in his biography of Alger, "each book bound him closer to the mediocrity he sought to avoid. Each book made it less possible for him to accomplish the ambition of his life." He worked hard and tirelessly, often ten or twelve hours at a stretch. He started *The Young Miners* on November 22, 1878, and had the completed manuscript in the publisher's hands by Christmas. Here is a small sample of Alger's writing taken from *Ragged Dick:* The thirteen-year-old Frank Whitney is talking to Ragged Dick:

> "You began in the right way when you determined never to steal or do anything mean or dishonorable, however strongly tempted to do so. That will make people have confidence in you when they come to know you. But, in order to succeed well, you must manage to get as good an education as you can."
>
> "That is so," replied Dick, "I never thought how awful ignorant I was till now."
>
> "That can be remedied by perseverance," said Frank.

Alger was revered from coast to coast and had tremendous influence on the youngsters of the Eighties, Nineties and the early years of the Twentieth Century.

COMPLETE LIST OF ALGER BOOKS

1. Driven from Home
2. A Cousin's Conspiracy
3. Ned Newton
4. Andy Gordon
5. Tony, the Tramp
6. The Five Hundred Dollar Check
7. Helping Himself
8. Making His Way
9. Try and Trust
10. Only an Irish Boy
11. Jed, the Poorhouse Boy
12. Chester Rand
13. Grit, the Young Boatman
14. Joe's Luck
15. From Farm Boy to Senator
16. The Young Outlaw
17. Jack's Ward
18. Dean Dunham
19. Both Sides of the Continent
20. The Store Boy
21. In a New World
22. Slow and Sure
23. Walter Sherwood's Probation
24. The Trials and Triumphs of Mark Mason
25. The Young Salesman
26. Andy Grant's Pluck
27. Facing the World
28. Luke Walton
29. Strive and Succeed
30. From Canal Boy to President
31. The Erie Train Boy
32. Paul the Peddler
33. The Young Miner
34. Charlie Codman's Cruise
35. A Debt of Honor
36. The Young Explorer
37. Ben's Nugget
38. The Errand Boy
39. Frank and Fearless
40. Frank Hunter's Peril
41. Adrift in the City
42. Tom Thatcher's Fortune
43. Tom Turner's Legacy
44. Dan the Newsboy
45. Digging for Gold
46. Lester's Luck
47. Brave and Bold
48. A New York Boy
49. Bob Burton
50. The Young Adventurer
51. Julius, the Street Boy
52. Adrift in New York
53. Tom Brace
54. Struggling Upward
55. New York Telegraph Boy
56. Tom Tracy
57. The Young Acrobat
58. Bound to Rise
59. Hector's Inheritance
60. Do or Dare
61. The Tin Box
62. Tom the Bootblack
63. Risen from the Ranks
64. Shifting for Himself
65. Wait and Hope
66. Sam's Chance
67. Striving for Fortune
68. Phil the Fiddler
69. Paul Prescott's Charge
70. Mark Manning's Mission
71. Rupert's Ambition
72. Sink or Swim
73. The Backwoods Boy
74. Tom Temple's Career
75. Ben Bruce
76. The Young Musician

77. The Telegraph Boy
78. Work and Win
79. The Train Boy
80. The Cash Boy
81. Herbert Carter's Legacy
82. Strong and Steady
83. Lost at Sea
84. From Farm to Fortune
85. Young Captain Jack
86. Joe, the Hotel Boy
87. Out of Business
88. Falling in with Fortune
89. Nelson, the Newsboy
90. Randy of the River
91. Jerry, the Backwoods Boy
92. Ben Logan's Triumph
93. The Young Book Agent
94. Luck and Pluck
95. Ragged Dick
96. Fame and Fortune
97. The Young Entertainer
98. Sandy Stone
99. Ben Barton's Battle
100. The Last Word
101. Tom Turner
102. Plan and Prosper
103. Cal Cooper's Triumph
104. Mark, the Match Boy
105. In Search of Treasure
106. Frank Starr's Purpose
107. Up the Ladder
108. Hobart, the Hired Boy
109. Ben, the Luggage Boy
110. Rufus and Rose
111. Rough and Ready
112. Ned Nestor's Plan
113. The Young Soldier
114. Toward the Top
115. Dean Dexter
116. Frank's Campaign
117. Bernard Brook's Adventures
118. Robert Coverdale's Struggles
119. The Making of a Man

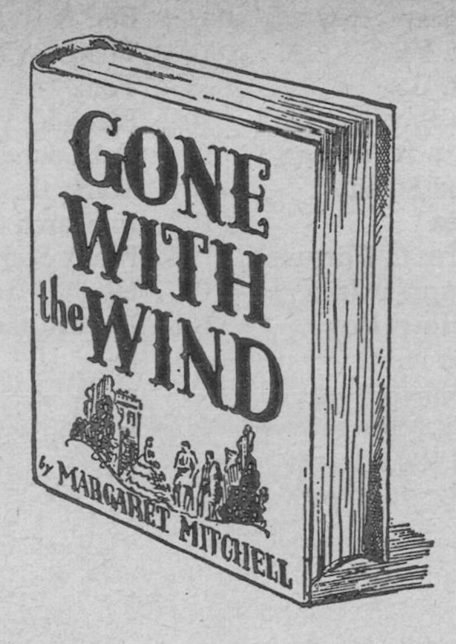

The Best-selling Novel of All Time

IN THE FALL OF 1935 MR. H. S. LATHAM, VICE-president of The Macmillan Company, was in Atlanta, Georgia. There Margaret Mitchell and Mrs. Medora Perkerson invited him to dinner. During the course of the meal Mrs. Perkerson said in an offhand way to Mr. Latham, "Peggy has written a book," and Mr. Latham expressed a desire to see it. But Miss Mitchell was too bashful at first and made light of the matter, saying that she was really not finished with it.

Before Mr. Latham returned to New York Miss Mitchell changed her mind and delivered the enormous manuscript to him. It was so bulky that Latham had to buy a new suitcase especially for it.

A few days after returning to New York Latham wired Miss Mitchell that Macmillan had accepted the manuscript and there would have to be a number of revisions. After working for six months on these the job was ready for the press and on June 30, 1936, it appeared in the bookstores.

Gone With the Wind started selling right away and as the days passed the sales mounted and mounted.

Everybody everywhere either bought it or got it from a lending library. In a single day more than 50,000 copies of this novel were sold. It was the July, 1936, selection of the Book-of-the-Month Club. Three weeks after publication 176,000 copies had been printed. By November, 1936, its sale had reached 700,000 copies and a year after it was published 1,375,000 copies had been sold—the largest sale of any novel during the first year.

Up and up went the sales of *Gone With the Wind*, week after week, month after month and year after year. By the fall of 1949 the 65th edition came off the press and the total sales had reached an all-time high, outselling all other novels of this century, with more than 6,000,000 copies in 30 languages and in 40 countries. Miss Mitchell became independently wealthy from the royalties, the movie rights, the reprint rights, the syndicate rights, and so on. This was her first and last novel for she was struck by an automobile near her home in Atlanta and died on August 16, 1949, as a result of her injuries.

Gone With the Wind was probably the best-selling novel of all time but this is difficult to prove. How many copies of *Vanity Fair* or *David Copperfield* or any of the other classics have been sold is anyone's guess. Nobody knows, but we do know that Miss Mitchell's novel was the most powerful best seller this century has seen—and it is still selling well today.

The Sháhnáma— Longest Poem by One Man

THE LONGEST POEM EVER WRITTEN BY ONE MAN IS *The Sháhnáma* of Firdâusi. Firdâusi was a Persian poet (A.D. 940-1020) who spent thirty-five years of his life writing this epic, known as the Book of Kings. It occupies 9 large volumes with a total of 2,804 pages and contains 60,000 couplets or 120,000 lines, which tell of the ancient kings of Persia—the story of the Pishdádian, Kaianian and Sasánian dynasties—and contains much philosophy and Persian folklore.

There is an interesting story connected with *The Sháhnáma*. The Sultan Mahmud who promised Firdâusi one gold piece for each couplet he wrote was influenced by his courtiers to substitute 60,000 silver pieces. When they were brought to Firdâusi he flatly refused them and wrote a vitriolic satire, considered one of the severest reproaches ever written. This naturally angered the Sultan, who condemned Firdâusi to death. But Firdâusi fled from the country and could not be found. Years later, at the age of eighty, he returned, and the Sultan, upon hearing this, decided to forgive him and let him have the gold he had promised. The story did not have a happy ending, however, because the elephant bearing the Sultan's gold met the funeral procession bearing the body of old Firdāusi.

The Sháhnáma was translated into English by Arthur and Edward Warner in 1905. This was a colossal job. In the first of the 9 large volumes there is an introduction of 87 pages and in the last volume we find an index and an analysis of the contents that takes up 280 pages. Says Edward Warner in the preface: "To the vast majority of English readers *The Sháhnáma* seems hardly to be known even by name—a fact not to be wondered at considering how few references are made to it in current literature and that this is actually the first attempt to give the subject matter of the great Persian epic at large in English."

Of course both of these tremendous poems are in blank verse and probably not one person in 10,000 has ever read either of them from cover to cover.

A Book that Can Rest on a Cobweb

IN THE BODLEIAN LIBRARY AT OXFORD IS THE SMALLEST book in the world. It is a privately printed translation of Omar Khayyam's *Rubaiyat* (the chief parts) done by the Commonwealth Press in Worcester, Massachusetts.

The little book measures ¼ inch in height and 3/16 inch in width, which is a little less than an eighth the size of a postage stamp. The size of the text on its 34 pages is 3/32 inch by 5/32 inch and the book weighs 1½ grains, which equals 1/327 ounce. The type, of course, is too small for ordinary reading and so delicate was the typesetting job that it had to be done at night when vibrations from traffic and office machinery had ceased.

ACTUAL SIZE

THE
VVHOLE
BOOKE OF PSALMES
Faithfully
TRANSLATED *into* ENGLISH
Metre.

Whereunto is prefixed a discourse declaring not only the lawfullnes, but also the necessity of the heavenly Ordinance of singing Scripture Psalmes in the Churches of God.

Coll. III.
Let the word of God dwell plenteously in you, in all wisdome, teaching and exhorting one another in Psalmes, Himnes, and spirituall Songs, singing to the Lord with grace in your hearts.

Iames v.
If any be afflicted, let him pray, and if any be merry let him sing psalmes.

Imprinted
1640

$151,000 for One Book

WHAT BOOK BROUGHT THE HIGHEST PRICE AT AN auction sale? Most people would say the Gutenberg Bible, a copy of which sold for $106,000 in 1926.

But the Gutenberg Bible is not the highest-priced book. This honor goes to the Bay Psalm Book, which was the first book printed in the English colonies in America. Under the title "Whole Book of Psalms Faithfully Translated Into English Metre" this book was published in 1640 by the Stephen Daye Press in Cambridge, Massachusetts. It was the very first printing establishment in the new Bay Colony.

On January 28, 1947, at the Parke-Bernet Galleries in New York, the Bay Psalm book sold for the sum of $151,000. This is the highest price ever paid for any book. The bidding opened with $30,000 and rapid advances of $1,000 bids were made until $91,000 was reached. At this point all other bidders dropped out and Mr. Whitney and Joseph Fleming, Dr. Rosenbach's representative, were left to fight it out. Mr. Whitney finally dropped out and Dr. Rosenbach got the Bay Psalm Book for $151,000.

There are only 11 Bay Psalm Books in the world and 4 of them are in private hands. The history of the particular book that sold for $151,000 has been traced to 1758 when it was one of five stored in the steeple chamber of the Old South Church in Boston. There it remained until 1850 when it was exchanged with two other copies for "modern books." It was acquired in this fashion by Edward A. Crowinshield, who put it in his library. When the Crowinshield library was sold, the book was bought by Henry Stevens, who had it rebound in dark brown crushed levant morocco and sold it to George Brinley of Hartford, Connecticut, for 150 guineas (about $70). In 1879 Cornelius Vanderbilt bought it for $1,200 and it did not come up for auction again until 1947.

The Shortest Letter and One of the Longest Sentences Ever Written

VICTOR HUGO ALMOST SET THE WORLD'S RECORD for short letter writing. A month or so after the octavo edition of *Les Miserables* was published he wrote to his publisher the following:

?
Victor Hugo

Hurst & Blackett, the London publishers, not to be outdone by the master, produced the world's shortest letter when they wrote back to Hugo on the firm's letterhead:

and did not sign it. Nobody could write anything shorter that would convey any meaning.

But just to prevent anyone from getting the wrong idea about Victor Hugo, we reprint here what we believe to be one of the longest sentences ever written —by Hugo himself in *Les Miserables*. This enormous single sentence contains 823 words and is about 4,500 times as long as the letter he wrote to his publisher.

ONE OF THE LONGEST SENTENCES—823 WORDS—3 PAGES FROM VICTOR HUGO'S *Les Miserables*

Son of a father to whom history will certainly grant extenuating circumstances, but as worthy of esteem as his father was of blame; possessing all the private virtues and several of the public virtues; careful of his health, his fortune, his person, and his business affairs; knowing the value of a minute, but not always the value of a year; sober, serious, peaceful, and patient; a good man and a good prince; sleeping with his wife, and having in his palace lackeys whose business it was to show the conjugal couch to the citizens—a regular ostentation which had grown useful after the old illegitimate displays of the elder branch; acquainted with all the languages of Europe, and, what is rarer still, with all the languages of all the interests, and speaking them; an admirable representative of the "middle classes," but surpassing them, and in every way greater; possessing the excellent sense, while appreciating the blood from which he sprang, of claiming merit for his personal value, and very particular on the question of his race by declaring himself an Orleans and not a Bourbon; a thorough first prince of the blood, so long as he had only been Most Serene Highness, but a frank bourgeois on the day when he became His Majesty; diffuse in public, and concise in private life; branded as a miser, but not proved to be one; in reality, one of those saving men who are easily prodigal to satisfy their caprices or their duty; well read and caring but little for literature; a gentleman but not a cavalier; simple, calm, and strong; adored by his family and his household; a seductive speaker, a statesman who had lost his illusions, cold-hearted, swayed by the immediate interest, governing from hand to mouth; incapable of rancor and of gratitude; pitilessly employing superiorities upon mediocrities, and clever in confounding by parliamentary majorities those mysterious unanimities which growl hoarsely beneath thrones; expansive, at times imprudent in his expansiveness, but displaying marvelous skill in his imprudence; fertile in expedients, faces, and masks; terrifying France by Europe, and

Europe by France; loving his country undeniably, but preferring his family; valuing domination more than authority, and authority more than dignity; a temperament which has this mournful feature about it, that by turning everything to success it admits of craft and does not absolutely repudiate baseness, but at the same time has this advantage, that it preserves politics from violent shocks, the State from fractures, and society from catastrophes; minute, correct, vigilant, attentive, sagacious, and indefatigable; contradicting himself at times, and belying himself; bold against Austria at Ancona, obstinate against England in Spain, bombarding Antwerp and paying Pritchard; singing the Marseillaise with conviction; inaccessible to despondency, to fatigue, to a taste for the beautiful and ideal, to rash generosity, to Utopias, chimeras, anger, vanity, and fear; possessing every form of personal bravery; a general at Valmy, a private at Jemappes; eight times attacked by regicides, and always smiling; brave as a grenadier, and courageous as a thinker; merely anxious about the chances of European convulsion, and unfitted for great political adventures; ever ready to risk his life, but not his work; disguising his will in influence for the sake of being obeyed as an intellect rather than as king; gifted with observation and not with divination; paying but slight attention to minds, but a good judge of men—that is to say, requiring to see ere he could judge; endowed with prompt and penetrating sense, practical wisdom, fluent tongue, and a prodigious memory, and incessantly drawing on that memory, his sole similitude with Caesar, Alexander, and Napoleon; knowing facts, details, dates, and proper names, but ignorant of the various passions and tendencies of the crowd, the internal aspirations, and concealed agitation of minds—in one word, of all that may be called the invisible currents of consciences; accepted by the surface, but agreeing little with the lower strata of French society; getting out of scrapes by skill; governing too much and not reigning sufficiently; his own Prime Minister; excellent in the art of setting up the littleness of realities as an obstacle to the immensity of ideas; mingling with a true creative faculty of civilization, order, and organization, I do not know what pettifogging temper and chicanery; the founder of a family and at the same time its man-of-law; having something of Charlemagne and something of an attorney in him; but on the whole, as a lofty and original figure, as a prince who managed to acquire power in spite of the anxiety of France, and influence in spite of the jealousy of Europe —Louis-Philippe would be ranked among the eminent men of his age, and among the most illustrious governors known in history, if he had loved glory a little, and had a feeling for what is grand to the same extent that he had a feeling for what is useful.

823 words, 93 commas, 51 semicolons, 4 dashes.

A 220,000-line Poem

HOMER'S *Iliad* AND *Odyssey* ARE CONSIDERED TWO unusually long poems. There is, however, an ancient Indian epic known as *Mahabharata,* which is more than *eight times as long as the Iliad and Odyssey combined* and nearly four times as long as the entire Bible!

Mahabharata, "the longest poem in the world," takes up eighteen large volumes with a total of 5,400 pages. Its 110,000 couplets or 220,000 lines, divided into 2,009 chapters, tell the story of the descendants of King Bharata (the *Maha* in front means *great*) and the ancient India where they lived and ruled. The poem is a vast repository—"a jungle of information"—of Hindu traditional lore, philosophy and legend. While the Indian poet Vyasa had a great deal to do with the arrangement of this great work, it is really the product of many generations of Brahman writers through nearly a whole millennium.

Mahabharata was originally only 24,000 couplets long, but it gradually grew to its present length of 110,000 couplets. It was written between the years 400 B.C. and 150 B.C.

The World's Best-selling Book of All Time

EVERYONE KNOWS THAT THE BIBLE IS THE WORLD'S best seller and that no other book can even remotely approach the enormous sales of the Holy Scriptures. But not many of us know the statistics. For example: Since its formation in 1816 the American Bible Society has distributed more than 395,000,000 Bibles, the British Bible Society another 410,000,000 and the Bible Society of Scotland some 300,000,000. This makes a total distribution or sale of 1,105,000,000 Bibles exclusive of the many thousands of small stores and religious organizations. It is safe to say that more than a billion and a half Bibles have been sold since the beginning of the nineteenth century—and that is certainly a lot of books.

The entire Bible has been translated into 190 languages, the New Testament into an additional 245 languages and parts of the Bible such as the Gospels into 683 more languages, making a grand total of 1,118 different languages. The first book printed by movable type was the Latin Bible about the year 1455. Here are a few "longest," "shortest" and "mosts" of the Bible:

The longest verse is the 9th verse of the 8th Chapter of Esther.

The shortest verse is the 35th of the 11th Chapter of John.

The longest chapter is the 119th Psalm; the shortest the 117th Psalm.

The longest word in the Bible is in the 8th Chapter of Isaiah. It is Mahershalalhashbaz.

The word occurring most in the Bible is "and"—46,277 times.

The word occurring least is "reverend"—once.

The Bible contains 3,566,480 letters; 773,693 words; 31,102 verses; 1,189 chapters and 66 books.

Author of More Than 500 Novels

THERE IS LITTLE DOUBT THAT THE WORLD'S MOST prolific writer is Georges Simenon, whom André Gide has called "perhaps the greatest novelist in French literature today."

Simenon was born in Liège, Belgium, on February 13, 1903. At the age of seventeen he published his first book, and today he has more than 500 novels to his credit. Certainly any man who can turn out 10 novels a year for fifty years deserves to be called the most prolific writer in the world!

At nineteen Simenon went to Paris where he produced two hundred novels and short stories in the short time of ten years. Many of these were just "popular," turned out as "pot boilers" or "bread-winners" and written under a score of different pseudonyms. At the age of thirty he launched the "Inspector Maigret" series, which took so well that the slick magazines of this country translated them and had difficulty supplying the demand. For two years after his first detective novel appeared Simenon put pressure on himself and actually turned out one detective novel a month!

In 1934 Simenon gave up detective story writing temporarily and turned his attention to more serious literary work. He slowed down his pace somewhat and turned out an average of only four books a year instead of twelve.

Georges Simenon has been compared with Balzac, Faulkner and Dostoevsky. Forty-six of his novels have been made into motion pictures, and over fifty have been produced as television plays.

SPORTS

The Longest Ball Game in Baseball History

ON MAY 1, 1920, THE BOSTON BRAVES PLAYED THE Brooklyn Dodgers (Robins as they were called at that time) in Boston. Catcher Otto Krueger scored in the fifth for Brooklyn and Wally Cruise tied the score in the sixth for Boston. In the next three innings neither side got a run and from then on it was a battle never equaled in baseball history. To quote from the story in the *New York Times* the following morning: ". . . the oldest living man can remember nothing like it nor can he find anything in his granddad's diary worth comparison. Heart disease was the mildest complaint that grasped the spectators as they watched inning after inning slip away and the row of ciphers in the scoreboard slide over the fence and reach into the Fenway."

After the twenty-sixth inning had been played the game was called on account of darkness with the following box score:

BROOKLYN	AB	R	H	PO	A
Olsen 2b	10	0	1	6	9
Neis rf	10	0	1	9	0
Johnson 3b	10	0	2	3	1
Wheat lf	9	0	2	3	0
Myers cf	2	0	1	2	0
Hood cf	6	0	1	8	1
Konetv'y lb	9	0	1	30	1
Ward ss	10	0	0	5	3
Krueger c	2	1	0	4	3
Elliott c	7	0	0	7	3
Cadore p	10	0	0	1	13
	85	1	9	78	34

BOSTON	AB	R	H	PO	A
Powell cf	7	0	1	8	0
Pick 2b	11	0	0	5	10
Mann lf	10	0	2	6	0
Cruise rf	9	1	1	4	0
Holke lb	10	0	2	43	1
Boeckel 3b	11	0	3	1	7
Maran'le ss	10	0	3	1	9
O'Neil c	2	0	0	4	3
Christen'y	1	0	1	0	0
Gowdy c	6	0	1	6	1
Oeschger p	8	0	1	0	11
	85	1	15	78	42

Brooklyn:
0 0 0 0 1 0 0 0 0 0 0 0 0 0 0 0 0 0 0 0 0 0 0 0 0 0

Boston:
0 0 0 0 0 1 0 0 0 0 0 0 0 0 0 0 0 0 0 0 0 0 0 0 0 0

The two pitchers were the heroes of the game. Joe Oeschger and Leon Cadore went the entire distance (equal to three ordinary games) without showing any signs of weakness. As a matter of fact they each appeared to grow stronger as the innings piled up. With the exception of Boston's flare-up in the ninth and Brooklyn's flash in the seventeenth the two pitchers were always the masters of the situation.

The fans who were present at this marathon saw 170 men at bat and 156 put-outs. In the four and a half hours of play, only two men crossed home plate.

The Fastest Baseball Ever Thrown

HOW FAST DO YOU THINK A BASEBALL TRAVELS WHEN pitched from the pitcher's box to the catcher? Does it ever go as fast as 60 miles per hour? Could anyone throw it with that speed?

Atley Donald, a pitcher for the New York Yankees, threw the fastest ball ever recorded. This was in 1939 in the stadium at Cleveland. The ball traveled at the rate of 94.7 miles per hour as indicated by the speed meter. This is much faster than most crack express trains and nearly half again as fast as the average ball pitched in the average game. The nearest competitor to this was a ball thrown by Dee Miles of the Philadelphia Athletics. This was clocked at 92 miles per hour. The energy of these balls as they strike the catcher's mitt is about 250 foot-pounds.

The World's Record Fight Attendance

STRANGE AS IT MAY SEEM TO MANY SPORT FANS, the largest attendance at a boxing bout was *not* at the famous Tunney-Dempsey Heavyweight Championship fight at Soldier Field in Chicago on September 22, 1927. That fight drew the highest gate in fistic history, $2,658,660, with an attendance of 104,943.

The record attendance for any boxing bout was 135,-132, according to the *Ring Record Book* of Nat Fleischer. This took place on August 18, 1941, in Milwaukee at the Fraternal Order of Eagles Free Show. This enormous crowd at Juneau Park saw Tony Zale fight and defeat Billy Pryor and add another victory to his middleweight title career.

110 Rounds to No Decision

PROBABLY EVERY SPORT FAN HAS HEARD OF THE FAmous Andy Bowen-Jack Burke fight that took place in New Orleans, April 6-7, 1893. It lasted for nearly seven and a half hours (9:15 P.M. to 4:34 A.M.) and went to 110 rounds to distinguish itself as the longest fight in all ring history.

Unfortunately that was the only distinction this fight had, for it was so dull that the referee, Jack Duffy, stopped it in the 110th round declaring it "no contest." Bowen, the black man, insisted on "fighting to the finish" but Duffy decided it was getting late and everyone wanted to go home. The write-up in the *Police Gazette* for April 7, 1893, tells the story well:

> THE LONG-WINDED BOWEN-BURKE FIGHT AT NEW ORLEANS
> The Bowen-Burke fight took place last Thursday night and Friday morning before several thousand spectators at the Olympic Club in New Orleans. It was stopped Friday morning in the 110th round by the referee, Jack Duffy, who decided that it was no contest. The purse will probably be divided. Bowen wanted to fight to a finish. The bones in both of Burke's hands were broken.
>
> Bowen, who is a New Orleans man, and Burke, a Texan, fought for a $2,500 purse, of which the loser was

to get $500, and the light-weight championship of the South. The betting previous to the fight favored New Orleans, and the largest crowd ever held by the Olympic Clubhouse was in attendance when the men entered the ring. That was at 9:30 o'clock Thursday night. In the twenty-fifth round Bowen was nearly knocked down and out by two punches on the head. His opponent failed to follow up his advantage.

Burke got a stiff punching in the twenty-eighth, and from then on up to the forty-fifth round the contest was dull and uninteresting. At the end of the forty-eighth Burke was knocked down and was only saved by the call of time for the interval between rounds. The crowd whistled "Home, Sweet Home," and at midnight many hundreds deserted the clubhouse for home. It was one of the poorest fights that had ever taken place in New Orleans, although both men were in perfect condition.

Skihistorics

IF YOU THINK THAT SKIS ARE FAIRLY MODERN, YOU are referred to the Nordiska Museum in Stockholm, Sweden. In one of their cases is a pair of skis that noted archeologists agree are not less than 4,000 years old. They are crude affairs, not like the skis we know today, but they are skis, nevertheless, and the oldest skis in the world.

The earliest recorded competition in skiing was among the military men of Oslo, Norway, in 1767.

The highest speed achieved by a skier is 109.14 mph by Ralph Miller (U.S.) at Portillo, Chile, on August 25, 1955.

Sports Superlatives

ON THE FOLLOWING PAGES ARE RECORDED SOME OF the greatest achievers and achievements in the world of sports through the first 70 years of the twentieth century. A survey has been taken of leading experts to prepare this final listing. The balloting was brisk and spirited in most instances.

In January, 1950, the Associated Press polled 393 of the nation's sports experts in order to compile a list of outstanding accomplishments and personalities in all fields of athletics for the first half of the century.

A summary of the 1950 balloting is also included here for the basis of comparison with the new list, which includes records through 1970.

Best Woman Athlete

THERE ARE MORE WOMEN COMPETING IN SPORTS than ever before in history, and the list keeps growing. The 1960's saw women competing with men as jockeys for the first time, and the ladies accorded themselves well. Most of the leading ladies in sports have come from the worlds of track, golf, and tennis. The outstanding female athlete of all time excelled in two of these, track and golf.

Here's the all-time list of top women athletes:

Mildred Didrikson (Babe) Zaharias
Margaret Court, Tennis, Australia
Chi Cheng, Track, China
Wilma Rudolph, Track, United States
Billie Jean King, Tennis, United States

BORN AT PORT ARTHUR, TEXAS, ON JUNE 26, 1912, Mildred Ella Didrikson became a top golf champion at the age of nineteen. In that year (1931) 250 of the country's leading women athletes met at Evanston, Illinois, for the national field and track meet and places on the United States Olympic Team. For two and a half hours Miss Didrikson amazed the spectators by winning seven first places, one tie for first place and one for second place. No other woman before or since has ever equaled her remarkable records in baseball, basketball, track and golf. In track she won 92 medals in two years and was the individual star at the 1932 Olympics at Los Angeles. Called by her family by the pet name of "Baby" she took on the name of "Babe" after hitting one home run after another in her high school games. She could throw a baseball record distances for a woman. She won 15 consecutive golf tournaments (1946) and was best known as the nation's leading professional woman golfer.

MARGARET COURT: Tall, graceful and beautiful, this Australian Amazon captured the Grand Slam of major international tournaments in 1970, the grandest achievement of a fabulously successful career on the courts. Her serve compares favorably with many men's in terms of power and her coverage of the court is relentless. After conquering the world of amateur ladies' tennis in the early 1960's, she retired for more than a year, but missed playing too much and came back. It wasn't long before she regained her place at the top.

Here are the results of the 1950 voting:

361 SPORTS EXPERTS VOTING

1. Mildred Zaharias (Babe Didrikson) ______319 votes
2. Helen Wills Moody (tennis) ____________ 25 votes
3. Stella Walsh (track) __________________ 10 votes
4. Fanny Blankers-Koen (Olympic star) ____ 7 votes

Baseball

THE YEAR 1969 MARKED THE 100TH ANNIVERSARY of professional baseball, or since the Cincinnati Red Stockings got the whole thing started in 1869. A nationwide poll was conducted to determine the greatest players at each position for the first century of the game's existence.

Not surprisingly, all the players who won the majority of votes at their position played exclusively in the 1900's, with the exception of Honus Wagner, who began his phenomenal shortstopping career before the turn of the century, but developed into an immortal of the game thereafter.

In addition to the poll by positions, the winners of which were honored at a midsummer banquet in Washington, D.C., on the eve of the 1969 All-Star Game, a vote was conducted to determine the greatest player of all time. It was a two-man contest all the way, as expected, with Babe Ruth, the New York Yankees' "Sultan of Swat" finally earning the accolade over Ty Cobb, the "Georgia Peach" of the Detroit Tigers. In AP's 1950 poll to determine the best baseball player of the first half of this century, Ruth and Cobb also ran well ahead of everyone else, Ruth winning.

Here are the players elected the best at their positions for the first century of baseball:

		GAMES	HITS	HR	B.A.
First base	Lou Gehrig	2163	2721	493	.340
Second base	Rogers Hornsby	2259	2930	302	.358
Third base	Pie Traynor	1961	2416	58	.320
Shortstop	Honus Wagner	2787	3415	101	.327
Catcher	Mickey Cochrane	1482	1652	119	.320
Outfield	Babe Ruth	2502	2873	714	.342
Outfield	Ty Cobb	3034	4192	118	.367
Outfield	Joe DiMaggio	1736	2214	369	.325

	GAMES	W	L	ShO	ERA
Pitcher (right-handed)					
Walter Johnson	802	413	277	110	2.17
Pitcher (left-handed)					
Lefty Grove	616	300	140	32	3.06

BABE RUTH: Born in Baltimore on February 6, 1895. Died in the Memorial Hospital in New York, August 16, 1948. No player in the history of the game had such an enormous influence on it as the Babe. No other man in baseball ever hit 714 home runs, 60 of them in one season. Few others were as well loved as this colorful and glamorous personality. Ruth was home run champion for 12 years: 1918, 1919, 1920, 1921, 1923, 1924, 1926, 1927, 1928, 1929, 1930, 1931. He holds the record for the greatest number of bases on balls—2,056, the greatest number of runs batted in—2,216, and, unofficially, the longest home run, which was hit in Tampa, Florida, and traveled 587 feet (nearly 2½ New York City blocks).

TY COBB: Ty Cobb was born in Banks County, Georgia, on December 17, 1886, and died on July 17, 1961, in Atlanta. He was 12 times batting champion, from 1907 to 1919 inclusive (with the exception of 1916), and leads all players in average, games, hits, runs, and stolen bases. He was at bat a record 11,437 times.

COMPARATIVE RECORDS

	G	AB	R	H	HR	2B	3B	%	YRS
RUTH	2502	8399	2174	2873	714	506	136	.342	22
COBB	3034	11437	2245	4192	118	725	294	.367	24

Here's the way they voted in 1950:

1. George Herman (Babe) Ruth
N.Y. Yankees (outfielder) ______ 253 votes
2. Tyrus Cobb
Detroit Tigers (outfielder) ______ 116 votes
3. Lou Gehrig
New York Yankees ______ 8 votes
4. Walter Johnson
Washington Senators ______ 7 votes
5. Joe DiMaggio
New York Yankees ______ 5 votes

Tennis

WHEN RODNEY GEORGE LAVER, THE RED-HEADED Australian left-hander, won all four major international amateur tennis tournaments—American, English, French and Australian—in 1962, he became only the second player in history to turn the trick. Don Budge was the first in 1938.

Shortly after his "Grand Slam" of 1962, Laver joined the ranks of professional tennis, which at that time still was a completely different game. With the arrival of "open tennis" in 1968, Laver was able to play in the major international tournaments once again. And in 1969 he scored an unprecedented second "Grand Slam" to cement his role as the finest tennis player of the twentieth century.

Laver narrowly edged Bill Tilden, U.S. champion six times, in the balloting. Here's how the top five finished:

Rod Laver, Australia
Bill Tilden, United States
Don Budge, United States
Pancho Gonzalez, United States
Ken Rosewall, Australia

ROD LAVER: Born in Rockhampton, Queensland, Australia, on August 9, 1938. An amazing left-hander with power and touch in perfect combination, despite deceptively small build. In addition to his four "Grand Slam" victories in 1952, he also won Italian and German championships that year. He has captured the All-England Championship (Wimbledon) four times, twice as an amateur, 1961 and 1962; twice as a pro, 1968 and 1969. He is equally proficient on all surfaces, indoors and outdoors.

Here are the results of the 1950 voting:

391 SPORTS EXPERTS VOTING

1. Bill Tilden	*310 votes*
2. Jack Kramer	*32 votes*
3. Don Budge	*31 votes*
4. Helen Wills Moody	*12 votes*
5. Suzanne Lenglen	*2 votes*

BILL TILDEN: He was the greatest tennis champion of his time, the early and middle twenties. William T. Tilden, II, won the United States men's singles championship in 1921, 1922, 1923, 1924, 1925 and 1929. In 1921, 1922, 1923 and 1927 he won in the men's doubles and the old-timers who saw "Big Bill" in action have never forgotten him. He had full command of every shot, and boasted a cannonball service, an acute command of tactics, and a fine match temperament. Tilden was born in Philadelphia on February 10, 1893, and died on June 5, 1953.

Ice Hockey

THE NATIONAL HOCKEY LEAGUE WAS ORGANIZED IN Montreal on November 22, 1917, and has been the chief professional hockey league since the 1920's. The Stanley Cup, awarded each spring to the winner of a series of playoffs between designated teams finishing highest during the regular season, is emblematic of hockey supremacy. The Montreal Canadiens, with 15 titles, have won more Stanley Cups than any other team, and have been represented by numerous outstanding stars over the years.

Here are the selections of the greatest performers ice hockey has seen:

FORWARDS

Gordie Howe
Bobby Hull
Maurice Richard

DEFENSEMEN

Eddie Shore
Doug Harvey
Bobby Orr

GOALTENDERS

Terry Sawchuk
Glenn Hall
Jacques Plante

GORDIE HOWE: Born in Floral, Saskatchewan, on March 31, 1928. The powerful right-winger of the Detroit Red Wings, who played his 25th season in the National Hockey League in 1970-71, holds virtually every meaningful record in the books—most goals, most assists, most points, most games played and, of course, most seasons of competition. Of the dozen or so records he holds, he is most proud of his longevity. Howe has won the NHL scoring title and been named the league's Most Valuable Player six times. Entering the 1970-71 season, he had 763 career goals.

EDDIE SHORE: Born in St. Qu'Appelle-Cupar, Saskatchewan, on November 25, 1902. "The Babe Ruth of Hockey" and the sport's greatest performer during most of the period he played, 1926-40, all but the last season with the Boston Bruins. Scored 105 goals, but was a fearsome and bruising body-checker, who dealt out awesome punishment. He could skate faster than most forwards too. He truly was "Mr. Defense."

TERRY SAWCHUK: Born, Winnipeg, Manitoba, on December 28, 1929. Died in New York City on May 31, 1970, of injuries received in a freak accident. Played more games, more seasons and recorded by far the most shutouts of any goaltender in history. Spent 13 of his 21 NHL seasons with Detroit, also starred for Boston, Toronto, Los Angeles and New York, for whom he was a substitute the season before he died. His career goals-against average was an incredible 2.52 and he posted 103 shutouts in regular-season competition and 12 more in Stanley Cup play. Four of those, and three in succession, came during the 1952 playoffs when he led the Red Wings to the championship in the minimum eight games, allowing only five goals in all.

Football (College)

WHEN COLLEGE FOOTBALL MARKED ITS 100TH ANniversary in 1969, a century after Princeton and Rutgers met in the first intercollegiate grid clash on November 6, 1869, a panel of past presidents of the Football Writers Association of America was asked to help commemorate the centennial by selecting two all-time teams—an Early Day team for the first 50 years (1869-1919), and a Modern team (1919-69). Nominations came from veteran writers and conference information directors in every region of the country.

There were three unanimous selections—Carlisle halfback Jim Thorpe and Yale guard Pudge Heffelfinger to the Early Day team, and Illinois halfback Red Grange to the Modern team.

Here are the players selected to the two all-time college football squads:

Early Day (1869-1919)

End	Frank Hinkey, Yale
End	Huntington Hardwick, Harvard
Tackle	Wilbur (Fats) Henry, Washington & Lee
Tackle	Josh Cody, Vanderbilt
Guard	Pudge Heffelfinger, Yale
Guard	T. Truxton Hare, Pennsylvania
Center	Adolph (Germany) Schultz, Michigan
Quarterback	Walter Eckersall, Chicago
Halfback	Jim Thorpe, Carlisle
Halfback	Willie Heston, Michigan
Halfback	Elmer Oliphant, Purdue and Army

JIM THORPE: Born in Prague, Oklahoma Territory, on May 28, 1886. The Sac and Fox Indian was named the greatest all-round athlete for the first 50 years of the century. In addition to his gridiron exploits, he excelled in track and field at the Stockholm Olympics in 1912, and played major league baseball. But he was best known for his football accomplishments, which were many. He played at the Carlisle Indian School in Pennsylvania in 1907, 1908, 1911 and 1912, compiling nearly 4,000 yards in rushing, including 362 in one 1912 game against Penn. He also scored 28 touchdowns that year. A 6-foot-2 giant, Thorpe was an early leader in pro football, serving the infant National Football League as its first president in 1920. He also was the pro game's first gate attraction. Thorpe died, a lonely, broken man, too fond of alcohol, in 1953. A town in Pennsylvania now carries his name.

Modern (1919-69)

End	Bennie Oosterbaan, Michigan
End	Don Hutson, Alabama
Tackle	Bronko Nagurski, Minnesota
Tackle	Frank (Bruiser) Kinard, Mississippi
Guard	Jim Parker, Ohio State
Guard	Bob Suffridge, Tennessee
Center	Mel Hein, Washington State
Quarterback	Sammy Baugh, Texas Christian
Halfback	Jay Berwanger, Chicago
Halfback	Red Grange, Illinois
Fullback	Ernie Nevers, Stanford

RED GRANGE: A Wheaton, Illinois, native who, at 125 pounds, was too small for his high school team, became a football legend as "Old number 77" during the 1923, 1924 and 1925 seasons at the University of Illinois. Primarily known for his running, he also was an expert passer and could punt and drop kick. During 20 collegiate games in three years he averaged 103.6 rushing yards per contest, with a high of 237 yards against Penn in 1925. His best game, however, and the one he is best remembered for, was against Michigan in 1924. In leading a 39-14 Illinois rout, he scored four touchdowns in the first 12 minutes, on a 95-yard kickoff return and runs of 67, 56 and 44 yards. Later in the game he scored a fifth TD and passed for still another, accounting for 402 total yards, 212 on the ground. Upon graduation from Illinois, he signed the largest professional football contract known to that time, helping establish the credibility of the pro game, which had many skeptics.

In 1970, the American Broadcasting Company, which telecasts college football nationally, conducted a poll of sportswriters and broadcasters to determine the top players of the 1960's. The results were as follows:

OFFENSE

O. J. Simpson, Southern California halfback
Roger Staubach, Navy quarterback

DEFENSE
Dick Butkus, Illinois linebacker
George Webster, Michigan State linebacker

O. J. SIMPSON: Played only two varsity years of varsity football (he spent two years in junior college) but rewrote collegiate rushing records in 19 games at the University of Southern California during 1967 and 1968. He led the nation in ground-gaining both years, with a record of 1,709 yards in 1968, and ran for 3,124 yards in all, a per-game average of 164.4, best mark in history. The 6-foot-2, 205-pound native of San Francisco also scored 33 touchdowns in his two varsity years. Simpson won the Heisman Trophy as college football's outstanding performer, in 1968, after finishing second in the 1967 balloting.

ROGER STAUBACH: One of the few lower classmen ever to win the Heisman Trophy, the great Navy quarterback won it in 1963 as a junior. He established an all-time record by completing 63.1 percent of his passes during his three varsity years. The 6-foot-2, 190-pound native of Cincinnati also was an excellent runner. After graduation from the Naval Academy, he was on active duty for four years.

DICK BUTKUS: A virtually unanimous All-America selection at center his last two years at the University of Illinois, 1963 and 1964, Butkus was best known for his fierce tackling, which helped Illinois earn a Rose Bowl berth on New Year's Day, 1964.

GEORGE WEBSTER: A key man on Michigan State's record-setting defensive units of 1965 and 1966, Webster functioned as a "rover back," covering runs and passes equally well. Webster was a unanimous All-America choice his last two years.

Football (Professional)

WHEN THE NATIONAL FOOTBALL LEAGUE MARKED its 50th anniversary in 1970, the Pro Football Hall of Fame in Canton, Ohio was called upon to compile a list of the league's greatest all-time players by positions. After consulting sports experts from coast to coast, the Pro Football Hall of Fame came up with this list:

Quarterback	Johnny Unitas
Fullback	Jim Brown
Halfback	Gale Sayers
Flanker	Elroy "Crazy Legs" Hirsch
Split end	Don Hutson
Tight end	John Mackey
Tackle	Cal Hubbard
Guard	Jerry Kramer
Center	Chuck Bednarik
Defensive end	Gino Marchetti
Defensive tackle	Leo Nomellini
Linebacker	Ray Nitschke
Cornerback	Dick "Night Train" Lane
Safety	Emlen Tunnell
Placekicker	Lou Groza

JOHNNY UNITAS: Born in Pittsburgh, Pennsylvania, on May 7, 1933, came off the sandlots of Pittsburgh and a mediocre college career at the University of Louisville to establish the most important career passing records in pro ball with the Baltimore Colts. He celebrated his 15th season in the pros by leading the Colts to the 1970 American Football Conference championship and into the Super Bowl. After 15 seasons his records included 4,777 passing attempts; 2,616 pass completions, 37,715 passing yards, and 280 touchdowns.

JIM BROWN: Born in St. Simons, Georgia, February 17, 1936. The greatest running back in pro football history, Brown possessed both speed and power in large quantities, moving like a halfback despite packing 232 pounds. He grew up in Manhasset, New York, and attended Syracuse University, where he gained All-America honors in both football and lacrosse. In three seasons of football at Syracuse, 1954-56, he gained 2,091 yards, averaging 6.2 yards per carry to lead the nation in 1956. In nine fabulous years, 1957-65, with the Cleveland Browns, he led the league in rushing every year except 1962, and surpassed the 1,000-yard mark seven times. His high was a record 1,863 yards in 1963. When he retired to launch a movie career following the 1965 season, Brown left behind a record of 12,312 rushing yards and 106 touchdowns.

The 1950 poll by the Associated Press to name football's best player of the first half of the twentieth century didn't differentiate between pro and college football, but all five players cited were honored largely for their collegiate achievements. Here they are:

391 SPORTS EXPERTS VOTING

1. James Thorpe *Carlisle, halfback*	*170 votes*
2. Harold (Red) Grange *Illinois, halfback*	*138 votes*
3. Bronko Nagurski *Minnesota, tackle*	*38 votes*
4. Ernie Nevers *Stanford, fullback*	*7 votes*
5. Sammy Baugh *Texas Christian, quarterback*	*7 votes*

Boxing

ALTHOUGH BOXING IS REPUTED TO HAVE BEEN IN somewhat of a decline the past two decades, there have been some commanding figures in the sport who have kept public interest at a high level. Though there are not as many fight broadcasts or telecasts as there once were, the advent of closed-circuit television in theaters and cable television has created some of the largest fight paydays in history. Here are three fighters who best bridged the gap between the old era of boxing and the modern epoch:

Sugar Ray Robinson
Muhammad Ali (Cassius Clay)
Rocky Marciano

SUGAR RAY ROBINSON: Born, Detroit, Michigan, on May 3, 1920. In a pro career spanning a quarter of a century, "Sugar" Ray won the world's welterweight championship and the middleweight crown a record five times. One of the most popular stylists in boxing annals, he turned pro in 1940 after winning Golden Gloves titles in 1939 as a featherweight and in 1940 as a lightweight. Robinson won the world's welterweight title by beating Tommy Bell in 15 rounds on

December 20, 1945. He first won the middleweight title by knocking out Jake LaMotta in 13 rounds on Valentine's Day, 1951. On June 25, 1952, he went after Joey Maxim's light-heavyweight championship in an outdoor fight in New York. Though ahead on points, Ray wilted in the heat and suffered the only knockout defeat of his career. He finally retired in November, 1965, after losing a close decision to middleweight contender Joey Archer. In 202 bouts, Robinson recorded 175 victories—109 by knockout—lost 19 times and was involved in six draws. Two of his bouts were ruled no contests.

MUHAMMAD ALI (CASSIUS CLAY): Born in Louisville, Kentucky, on January 17, 1942. Captured Olympic light-heavyweight crown at Rome in 1960, and four years later, at age 22, stunned the sports world by winning the world title from a supposedly invincible Sonny Liston, when the latter failed to answer the bell for the seventh round. Ali was involved in many controversies because of his affiliations with alleged "hate" groups, but was very popular with the fans. After knocking out Zora Folley in Madison Square Garden in April, 1967, for his ninth title defense, he refused to enter the Army, whereupon his title was stripped from him. He was finally reinstated following several court battles, and knocked out Jerry Quarry and Oscar Bonavena in late 1970 fights to move close to reclaiming the top rung in the boxing ladder.

ROCKY MARCIANO: Born in Brockton, Massachusetts, on September 1, 1923. Real name, Rocco Marchegiano. Killed in plane crash near Newton, Iowa, en route from Des Moines to Chicago on August 29, 1969. At the time of his death Marciano was awaiting the results of the computerized filmed "fight" he had staged with Ali to determine an all-time heavyweight champion. During his true-life ring career, Rocky never lost in 49 bouts, between 1947 and 1955. After quelling light-heavyweight champion Archie Moore's bid for the heavyweight title by knocking out Moore in 8 rounds, September 17, 1955, Marciano retired undefeated and never fought again. He earned the title with a crushing 13-round knockout of Jersey Joe Walcott, on September 23, 1952. Oh yes, he also defeated Ali in the computer fight 17 years later, though he was fated never to know.

Here's the way the Associated Press poll of 1950 listed the great fighters of the first half of the twentieth century:

393 SPORTS EXPERTS VOTING

1. William Harrison (Jack) Dempsey	
Heavyweight	*251 votes*
2. Joe Barrow (Louis)	
Heavyweight	*104 votes*
3. Henry Armstrong	
Middleweight	*16 votes*
4. Gene Tunney	
Heavyweight	*6 votes*
5. Benny Leonard	
Lightweight	*5 votes*

JACK DEMPSEY: Born at Manassa, Colorado, on June 24, 1895, he started his fighting career in the mining camps of Utah and Colorado back in 1912. Dempsey was considered a fighter and not a boxer for he was merciless inside the ring. In his prime he may have been the most perfect fighting machine of all time, even surpassing Joe Louis at his best. The exhibition at Toledo on the hot afternoon of July 4, 1919, when Dempsey floored the giant Jess Willard seven times in the first round was one of the most dramatic highlights in all sports history. No fighter was as colorful and yet as raw and savage. Dempsey began fighting in 1914 under the name Kid Blackie and stayed active through 1932. After three comeback exhibition bouts in 1940 at age 45, he turned to refereeing. The "Manassa Mauler" was honored early in 1971 as "the greatest athlete of the twentieth century."

JOE LOUIS: Born on May 13, 1914, near Lexington, Alabama, full name Joe Louis Barrow. He defended his title more than any other champion in history, and of his 76 ring contests he won 64 times by KO, won 8 times by decision, once by a disqualification. He lost only three times, on knockouts to Max Schmeling and Rocky Marciano, and a 15-round decision to Ezzard Charles in a futile comeback try. Louis won the title by KOing Jimmy Braddock in 8 rounds in Chicago, on June 22, 1937. He made 25 consecutive successful defenses, including a dramatic one-round KO of Max Schmeling, his conqueror by knockout in 1936, on June 22, 1938. On March 1, 1949, Louis announced his retirement as undefeated heavyweight champion, but returned to the ring late in 1950. After being knocked-out in 8 rounds by up-and-coming Marciano on October 26, 1951, Louis retired for good.

Track and Field

CONTINUING TO DEFY EVEN THE MOST OPTIMISTIC experts, track and field records toppled in bushels during the 1960's, with such previously cherished barriers as the 17-foot pole vault, 9.3 100-yard dash, 70-foot shot put, and others left in ruins.

As of January 1, 1971, these were the world record performances in standard men's events:

Event	Time or Distance	Record-holder	Year
100 yards	9.1 sec.	Bob Hayes, U.S.	1963
	9.1 sec.	Harry Jerome, Can.	1966
	9.1 sec.	Jim Hines, U.S.	1967
	9.1 sec.	Charlie Greene, U.S.	1967
	9.1 sec.	John Carlos, U.S.	1969
220 yards	20.0 sec.	Tommie Smith, U.S.	1966
440 yards	44.7 sec.	Curtis Mills, U.S.	1969
880 yards	1:44.9	Jim Ryun	1966
1 Mile	3:51.1	Jim Ryun	1967
2 Miles	8:19.6	Ron Clarke, Aust.	1968
3 Miles	12:50.4	Ron Clarke, Aust.	1966
6 Miles	26:47.0	Ron Clarke, Aust.	1965
3000-meter steeplechase	8:22.0	Kerry O'Brien, Aust.	1970
120-yard high hurdles	13.2 sec.	Martin Lauer, W. Ger.	1959
	13.2 sec.	Lee Calhoun, U.S.	1960
	13.2 sec.	Earl McCullouch, U.S.	1967
	13.2 sec.	Erv Hall, Villanova	1969
	13.2 sec.	Willie Davenport, U.S.	1969
	13.2 sec.	Thomas Hill, U.S.	1970
440-yard intermediate hurdles	48.8 sec.	Ralph Mann, U.S.	1970
High Jump	7-6¼	Ni Chih-Chin, Com. China	1970
Pole Vault	18-0¼	Chris Papanicolaou, Greece	1970
Long Jump	29-2½	Bob Beamon, U.S.	1968
Triple Jump	57-0¾	Viktor Saneyev, U.S.S.R.	1968
Shot Put	71-5½	Randy Matson, U.S.	1967
Discus Throw	224-4¾	Jay Silvester, U.S.	1968
Hammer Throw	247-7½	Anatoly Bondarchuk, U.S.S.R.	1969
Javelin Throw	304-1½	Jorma Kinnunen, Finland	1969
Decathlon	817 pts.	Bill Toomey, U.S.	1969

BOB HAYES: This powerfully built athlete, who went on to pro football fame with the Dallas Cowboys, ruled the sprinting world through his four collegiate years at Florida A & M, 1961-64. In 62 finals at 100 yards or the slightly longer 100 meters, he lost only twice, and both of those in one week after he had been ill. Although he was not considered as strong as some starting out of the blocks, he was a tremendous finisher. Probably his greatest finish came as the anchor man of the U.S. 440-meter relay team at the Tokyo Olympics in 1964, when he got the baton in a trailing position. He poured on a tremendous effort which carried him well past the second-place man. He ran 100 yards in 9.3 seconds or less on 19 occasions, and was the first 9.1 sprinter at the AAU Championships in 1963 in St. Louis.

JIM RYUN: At 17 years old, in 1964, he became the youngest runner ever to run a mile in less than four minutes, 3:59.0, and later that year became the youngest track star ever to represent the United States in the Olympics. However, he wasn't at his best in Tokyo, because of illness. After the 1964 Olympics he quickly rose to the top of world mile-running. He enrolled at Kansas University, and early in 1966, at Terre Haute, Indiana, he unexpectedly broke the world 880-yard (half mile) record with a 1:44.9 clocking. Later that year, on July 17, at Berkeley, he broke the world record for the mile with a time of 3:51.3, taking more than two seconds off the listed mark of that time. At Bakersfield, California, on June 23, 1967, he lowered his mile record to 3:51.1. At the Mexico City Olympics in 1968, he ran 3:37.8 for 1,500 meters, faster than he had expected, but finished second to Kenya's Kipchoge Keino, who was at an advantage in the high altitude of Mexico City. In the summer of 1969, Ryun retired from track, many thought for good. But he began serious workouts again late in 1970 and returned to competition with a fine 4:04.4 indoor mile in January, 1971.

Though he has never held the world record in his specialty, another athlete who should be singled out for comment as an all-time great is—

AL OERTER: No man has ever dominated an event in the Olympics as has the Long Island native who captured the discus gold medal at four consecutive Olympics—1956, 1960, 1964 and 1968. He has won despite having to wear a back brace at Tokyo in 1964, and despite usually being considered an underdog. He won his fourth gold medal at Mexico City with the longest throw of his life—212 feet, 4½ inches, almost five feet farther than he had ever done. He hadn't even considered trying for a fourth Olympics the year before, when he had a poor competitive season.

The 1950 AP balloting for track went like this:

382 SPORTS EXPERTS VOTING

1. Jesse Owens	
Ohio State sprinter	*201 votes*
2. Jim Thorpe	
Carlisle decathlete	*74 votes*
3. Paavo Nurmi	
Finnish distance runner	*31 votes*
4. Glenn Cunningham	
distance runner	*30 votes*
5. Cornelius Warmerdam	
pole vaulter	*12 votes*

JESSE OWENS: He had the greatest hour in the history of track at the Big Ten championships at Ann Arbor, Michigan, on May 25, 1935. Competing for Ohio State, within the space of that hour, he (1) equaled the world record in the 100-yard dash, (2) broke the world long-jump record with a leap of 26 feet, 8¼ inches, a mark that was to stand for 25 years, (3) broke the world record for 200 meters and 220 yards in the same race and (4) broke the world record for the 220-yard low hurdles and 200-meter low hurdles in the same race. Five world records established and one tied in one hour! In the 1936 Olympics at Berlin, Germany, Owens won four gold medals, winning individual championships in the 100-meter dash, 200-meter dash and long jump, and running a leg on the U.S. 400-meter relay.

Swimming

THE ONLY WAY ANYBODY COULD LAY CLAIM TO HAVING a complete collection of swimming records would be for him to work at it every single day—and even then he would likely miss a record performance from somewhere in the world. No other sport produces such short-lived records as swimming, with new and faster 13- and 14-year-olds coming along almost daily to supplant yesterday's heroes, who have suddenly grown "old."

Here are three outstanding men and women swimmers whose achievements not only involved speed in swimming, but endurance over many races or many years.

MEN	WOMEN
Murray Rose, Australia	Debbie Meyer, U.S.
Don Schollander, U.S.	Dawn Fraser, Australia
Mark Spitz, U.S.	Karen Muir, South Africa

MURRAY ROSE: One of the strongest distance swimmers of all time, Rose, who went on to fame as a commentator and male model, captured the 400-meter free-style swim at both the 1956 and 1960 Olympics, also won the 1,500-meter free-style in 1956 and finished second in 1960. In each of his 400-meter victories, he broke the listed Olympic record.

Don Schollander: The toast of the Tokyo Olympics, the Oregon native captured four gold medals—in the 100- and 400-meter free-style, and in the 400- and 800-meter free-style relays. He returned for one last gasp at age 22 in 1968, where he qualified for the 200-meter free-style final, but was nosed out for the gold medal.

Mark Spitz: As of January 1, 1971, Spitz, a Californian attending Indiana University, held four world records—100- and 200-meter free-style, and 100- and 200-meter butterfly. He burst upon the international swimming scene as a 14-year-old at the World Maccabiah Games in Tel Aviv, Israel, in the summer of 1965, where he swam and won virtually everything in sight. Expected to have an outside chance for as many as six gold medals at the Mexico City Olympics, Spitz was a disappointment and failed to win an individual event, though he did capture two gold medals for being a member of winning relay teams. He also won one silver medal for a second place and a bronze medal for a third.

Debbie Meyer: No swimmer ever matched the haul of three gold medals in individual events that this 16-year-old managed at the Tokyo Olympics. She swept the 200-, 400- and 800-meter free-style events. Earlier in the Olympic year of 1968, she had blasted all the world's free-style records for women, and at the beginning of 1971 still held the world marks at 200, 400 and 1,500 meters.

Dawn Fraser: This magnificent Australian lady proved that even "old" ladies of 26 can win in Olympic swimming when she captured her third consecutive 100-meter free-style championship at Tokyo. She also won in 1956 and 1960, and in all three victories surpassed the Olympic record.

Karen Muir: Until she retired from competition in 1971, this powerful South African girl had been the leading female backstroker in the world practically from the age of 12, in 1965. Unfortunately, she never was able to test her skill against the world's best competition at the Olympics, because of the ban against her country. But she did beat many of the world's best in other meets.

The results of the 1950 AP poll in swimming:

234 SPORTS EXPERTS VOTING

1. Johnny Weismuller		*132 votes*
2. Hironoshin Furuhashi	*speed champ*	*40 votes*
3. Adolph Kiefer	*backstroke*	*11 votes*
4. Duke Kahanamoku		*10 votes*

JOHNNY WEISMULLER: He was to swimming what Jack Dempsey was to fighting. At one time he held 67 swimming records and had the distinction of setting world's records for the 100- and 400-meter free-style events for the United States in the 1924 Olympics at Paris and the 1928 Olympics at Amsterdam. The younger generation knows Weismuller as the great film star who played Tarzan and other wild parts.

Golf

THERE IS PROBABLY LESS DIFFERENCE BETWEEN THE greats of the past and present, and even between greats of a particular era, in golf than in any other sport. The difference in scores over a long period of time is usually so minute as to be absolutely inconclusive.

Who really is the best golfer of all time? Suffice it

to say that the sport came into its own as a major television vehicle during the ear when the following men were rising to greatness, and that these men both benefited, and were benefited by, golf's growth. Certainly a valid argument could be made that the best golfers of previous eras would have won just as much money, and received the same accolades as present-day golfers, had their situations been the same.

Here are the "big four" of the modern era of golf:

Arnold Palmer
Jack Nicklaus
Gary Player
Billy Casper

ARNOLD PALMER: Born in Latrobe, Pennsylvania, on September 10, 1929. One of the most popular and dynamic individuals in the history of all sports, Palmer's style and ability began attracting attention in the 1950's, and as he grew in stature, so did the size of "Arnie's Army," the omnipresent pack of fans who followed his every move on the course. Palmer won the Masters in 1958, 1960, 1962, 1964; the U.S. Open in 1960; and the British Open in 1961, 1962. Through 1970 Palmer had won 59 tournaments.

JACK NICKLAUS: Born in Columbus, Ohio, on January 21, 1940. He finished second in the U.S. Open as a 20-year-old amateur in 1960, then won the tournament in 1962 the first time he played it as a pro. A powerful hitter all over the course, Nicklaus broke Ben Hogan's 72-hole record with a 275 score at the U.S. Open in 1967, the other time he won that tournament. He also won the Masters in 1963, 1965 and 1966; the British Open in 1966; and the PGA in 1963. Through 1970 he had won 35 professional tournaments.

GARY PLAYER: Born in Johannesburg, South Africa, on November 1, 1935. Perhaps best known for donating to charity his entire $25,000 purse for winning the U.S. Open in 1965, Player is a physical-fitness advocate and is also known for wearing all-black golfer apparel during many of his tournaments. Along with Nicklaus, he is one of the few men in history to have at least one victory in each of golf's "Big Four" tournaments—the U.S. Open, Masters, PGA and British Open. Player won the British Open in 1959 and 1968; the U.S. Open in 1965; the Masters in 1961 and the PGA in 1962.

BILLY CASPER: Born in San Diego, California, on June 24, 1931. He was the leading money winner in 1966, 1968 and 1970, winning the Masters for the first time in the latter year, and taking over the top spot on the all-time winnings list. One of the most consistent scorers and money-winners in history, Casper never was worse than 12th in winnings for 14 straight years. He won the U.S. Open in 1959 and 1966. Once teased for being overweight, he claims he diets on buffalo meat for conditioning and to maintain a proper weight. Casper is regarded as perhaps the finest putter in history.

The Associated Press poll of 1950 uncovered five more names that would rank as superb golfers in any era:

392 SPORTS EXPERTS VOTING

1. Bobby Jones	*293 votes*
2. Ben Hogan	*40 votes*
3. Walter Hagen	*29 votes*
4. Byron Nelson	*17 votes*
5. Sammy Snead	*6 votes*

BOBBY JONES: Born in Atlanta, Georgia, on March 17, 1902. The greatest name in golf of his time Jones won every major championship from one to five times and then retired at the age of twenty-eight. In 1930 Jones climaxed his spectacular career by winning four top championships—the U.S. Open, U.S. Amateur, British Open and British Amateur, constituting the "Grand Slam"—in four months. He won 13 major championships in all. Here are a few of the honors he won:

Junior Championship of Atlanta at nine
Four championships in 1916 at fourteen
Southern Amateur, 1922
U.S. Open, 1924, 1927, 1930
U.S. Amateur, 1925, 1926, 1928, 1929, 1930
British Amateur, 1927, 1928, 1930

BEN HOGAN: Born in Dublin, Texas, on August 13, 1912. From 1940 through 1960, he never was out of the top ten in the U.S. Open, a remarkable enough achievement. Probably most remarkable about Hogan, however, was his recovery from a near-fatal automobile accident in 1949. He won six of his nine major titles, including the 1950, 1951 and 1953 U.S. Opens, following the accident.

Basketball (College)

SO PRONOUNCED HAS BEEN THE IMPROVEMENT IN basketball skills and statistics over the years that it is today considered doubtful that any of the top stars of 20 or 25 years ago could have competed against the modern players.

Take, for example, the upsurge in field goal percentages in just one generation. In 1951, the nation's college players hit a collective 33.1 per cent of their tries for baskets. In 1970 the figure was an all-time record of 44.2 percent.

Here are the top five college players of the 1951-70 period, as chosen by a nationwide panel of sports experts:

Lew Alcindor, UCLA
Bill Bradley, Princeton
Jerry Lucas, Ohio State
Pete Maravich, Louisiana State
Oscar Robertson, Cincinnati

All but Bradley, who was honored twice, were consensus All-America choices all three of their varsity seasons. A rundown of their records follows:

	Years	G	FG-FGA	FG%	FT-FTA	FT%	Reb.	Pts.	Avg.
Alcindor	1967-69	88	943-1476	.639	439- 699	.628	1367	2325	26.4
Bradley	1963-65	83	856-1667	.513	791- 903	.876	1008	2503	30.2
Lucas	1960-62	82	776-1243	.624	438- 564	.777	1411	1990	24.3
Maravich	1968-70	83	1387-3166	.438	893-1152	.775	528	3667	44.2
Robertson	1958-60	88	1052-1968	.535	869-1114	.780	1338	2973	33.8

PETE MARAVICH: Born in Aliquippa, Pennsylvania, on June 22, 1948. The most prolific point producer in college basketball history, Maravich established records for field goals made and attempted, free throws made and attempted, total points and scoring average. His single-season scoring averages were 43.8, 44.2 and 44.5, respectively. On 28 occasions this 6-foot-5 blond scored 50 or more points, and on December 22, 1969, established a record for one game by making 30 free throws in 31 attempts against Oregon State.

OSCAR ROBERTSON: Born in Charlotte, Tennessee, on November 24, 1938. The first player to lead the college scoring averages all three of his varsity seasons, graduated with career records in points and average, and single-season average of 35.1 points per game in 1958. The consummate tactician on the court, the 6-foot-5 Robertson went on to professional greatness with the Cincinnati Royals and Milwaukee Bucks.

LEW ALCINDOR: Born in New York City on April 16, 1947. During his three years there, UCLA basketball teams won 88 games and lost only two, and won three consecutive national championships. The 7-foot-2 giant established a career record in field goal percentage, leading the nation's college players in that category twice. As a sophomore he set the single-season record by hitting on 66.7 percent of his shots. After graduation, Alcindor went on to the NBA's Milwaukee Bucks.

Since pro basketball had not made much of a mark at the time of the Associated Press half-century poll in 1950, the voters concerned themselves with college players. Here's how that voting went:

380 SPORTS EXPERTS VOTING

1. George Mikan, DePaul	*139 votes*
2. Hank Luisetti, Stanford	*123 votes*

GEORGE MIKAN: The greatest "giant" of his time, at 6-foot-10, Mikan was a member of the Helms Foundation All-America team in 1944, 1945 and 1946. During his four-year playing career at DePaul University in Chicago, the team won 81 games and lost 17, and the bespectacled tall man scored 1,868 points for a 19.1 average. In later years he was the first polished big man of pro basketball, leading the Minneapolis Lakers to five championships in the six-year period, 1948-54.

HANK LUISETTI: A three-time Helms All-America, 1936-38, Luisetti is credited with ushering in the modern jump-shooting era, by developing the finest one-handed jumper of his era. Before Luisetti, virtually all players shot two-handed.

Basketball (Professional)

THE NATIONAL BASKETBALL ASSOCIATION ENLISTED the cooperation of the nation's leading sports experts to compile an All-Star Team to commemorate the league's 25th anniversary during the 1970-71 season. The All-Star team could not include active NBA players, so luminaries such as *Wilt Chamberlain, Oscar Robertson, Jerry West, Elgin Baylor* and many others were not eligible.

When the final 10-man squad was selected, it was announced that Bill Russell was the only unanimous selection. The entire squad was honored at the NBA's All-Star Game in San Diego, on January 12, 1971.

Here are the players named to the NBA's Silver Anniversary All-Star Team and their pro records:

	G	FG	FT	PTS.	AVG.
Paul Arizin	713	5,628	5,010	16,266	22.8
Bob Cousy	917	6,167	4,621	16,955	18.5
Bob Davies	569	2,720	2,331	7,771	13.7
Joe Fulks	489	2,824	2,355	8,003	16.4
Sam Jones	802	5,762	2,716	14,240	17.8
George Mikan	520	4,097	3,570	11,764	22.6
Bob Pettit	792	7,349	6,182	20,880	26.4
Bill Russell	963	5,687	3,148	14,522	15.1
Dolph Schayes	1,059	6,135	6,979	19,249	18.2
Bill Sharman	710	4,761	3,143	12,665	17.8

Modern professional basketball has been dominated by two players whose approaches to the sport were almost exactly opposite. One was Bill Russell, who led the Boston Celtics to 11 NBA championships in 13 seasons, the last three years as the team's player-coach. He revolutionized the game with his efforts on rebounding, in which he established a career record, and on defense. He intimidated legions of shooters with his fantastic reach and shot-blocking prowess.

The other dominant figure was Wilt Chamberlain, the greatest offensive force in the sport's annals. He established every point-scoring record, for game, season and career, and has the best shooting percentage of all time.

COMPARATIVE RECORDS

	G	FG-FGA	FG%	FT-FTA	FT%	Reb.	Pts.	Avg.
Russell	963	5687-12930	.440	3148- 5614	.561	26721	14522	15.1
Chamberlain*	799	11091-20943	.530	5244-10210	.514	19233	27426	34.3

* Figures are through the 1969-70 season.

BILL RUSSELL: Born in Monroe, Louisiana, on February 12, 1934. If one word could be used to sum up Russell's basketball career, that word would be "winning." At the University of San Francisco, the 6-foot-9 giant led his team to consecutive collegiate basketball titles in 1955 and 1956. From the Melbourne Olympics, he reported to the Boston Celtics, and he helped them win their first NBA crown in his very first season. He was injured before the final round in 1958, and the Celtics were beaten by St. Louis. But Russell led them to an incredible eight straight titles from that point. He was named to coach the team for the 1966-67 season, and though he fulfilled his role as player-coach well enough so that the Celtics won 60 and lost only 21, the Philadelphia 76ers chose that season to break the league mark with a 68-13 record. The 76ers also prevailed in the playoffs. After taking the Celtics to two more titles the next two years, Russell retired following the 1968-69 campaign.

WILT CHAMBERLAIN: Born in Philadelphia, Pennsylvania, on August 21, 1936. Disdaining his senior season at Kansas University after leading the team to a 42-8 record with a 29.9 scoring average his sophomore and junior years, 1957 and 1958, Chamberlain joined the NBA with the Philadelphia Warriors for the 1959-60 season. The Warriors had claimed him as a territorial draft choice even while Wilt was attending Philadelphia's Overbrook High School a few years earlier. He proceeded to win the NBA scoring title his first seven years in the league. Wilt "The Stilt" played for the Warriors in Philadelphia and after they moved to San Francisco in 1963. Then he was traded back to Philadelphia, to the 76ers, where he remained until 1969 when he was traded to the Los Angeles Lakers. While with the Warriors in the 1961-62 season, Chamberlain achieved what had been considered the ultimate in point production—100 points (36 field goals, 28 free throws) against the New York Knicks on March 2, 1962. That season Wilt scored 50 or more points in 45 games and averaged 50.4 points per contest. In 1966-67, as the leader of the 76er team that finally stopped the Celtics' long run of championships, Wilt established another record by sinking 68.3 percent of his shots. During one stretch of four games, he made 35 consecutive baskets, another record.

The Greatest Sports Upset

INCREDIBLY, WITHIN THE SPACE OF 10 MONTHS IN 1969, two New York teams recorded shocking victories over Baltimore teams, a pair of results that rank as the two most incredible in sports annals.

Here are five leading reversals of form that have occurred in modern sports:

New York Jets beat Baltimore Colts in Super Bowl, 1969.

New York Mets beat Baltimore Orioles in World Series, 1969.

Cassius Clay, a 7-1 underdog, knocks out Sonny Liston for world heavyweight championship.

Billy Mills wins Olympic 10,000-meter run for U.S. at Tokyo Olympics in 1964.

Boston Red Sox win American League pennant, 1967.

JETS BEAT COLTS: Joe Namath "guaranteed" his New York Jets would beat the supposedly unbeatable Baltimore Colts, champions of the proud National Football League, when the teams met to decide the championship of pro football on January 12, 1969. The Jets had won the American Football League title, but still were lightly regarded, and pre-game predictions had the Colts winning by as many as seven touchdowns. Then, before 75,377 fans in Miami's Orange Bowl, Namath made good his guarantee. He destroyed the vaunted Baltimore defense with his expert play-calling. By the time the Colts scored their only touchdown of the game in the fourth period, the Jets had counted three field goals by Jim Turner and a touchdown run by Matt Snell. Final score: Jets 16, Colts 7.

METS BEAT ORIOLES: The New York Mets, under manager Gil Hodges, fashioned a major miracle simply by winning the 1969 National League pennant as 100-1 underdogs. They had finished ninth in the 10-team league the previous season. When they squared off against the Baltimore Orioles, runaway victors of the American League flag, to decide the World Series, the Mets again were nearly prohibitive underdogs. After losing the first game, 4-1, the Mets seemed to be proving the experts right. Then, in a stunning and completely unexpected reversal of form, the New Yorkers ran off four victories in a row to claim the world title. They won the second game at Baltimore, 2-1, then, before their own deliriously happy fans at Shea Stadium, decided the issue with 5-0, 2-1 and 5-3 decisions. On October 16, 1969, the result was official: another New York team had clobbered another Baltimore team.

The 1950 balloting to determine the greatest upset in sports to that time resulted in the following decision:

361 SPORTS EXPERTS VOTING

1. The victory of the Boston Braves over the Athletics in 1914	*128 votes*
2. Tunney's defeat of Dempsey in the title bout of 1926	*53 votes*
3. Centre College's football victory over Harvard in 1921	*40 votes*
4. Braddock's defeat of Baer in the 1935 heavyweight title bout	*24 votes*

BY ALL ODDS THE GREATEST SPORTS UPSET OF THE first half of the twentieth century was the remarkable showing of the Boston Braves back in 1914. On July 9 of that year the Braves were in last place, 11½ games behind the first place New York Giants. After being in this discouraging position for 97 out of 100 days the Braves began to pick up. Up and up they went until, on August 8, they were in first place and a week or so later they won the National League pennant for the first time in their history. But that was not all. Under the direction of the great George Stallings, the Braves whitewashed the Athletics by winning four straight games in the World Series, thereby traveling from a hopeless position in the cellar of the league to the 1914 World Championship in two months. The heroes of that world champion team, which stunned the baseball world in that short series were Hank Gowdy, the catcher, Johnny Evers, the second baseman, and Rabbit Maranville, the shortstop. Gowdy hit .545 and Evers .438, and the proud Philadelphia team went down in utter defeat.

The Longest Throw in Baseball History

ON AUGUST 23, 1953, DON GRATE, ONCE AN OUTfielder of the Philadelphia Phillies, threw a baseball a distance of 443 feet, 3½ inches. In most ball parks it is equal to the distance from the center field bleachers fence to home plate. And that's some throw!

On August 18, 1957, Amelia Wershoven established a record for women by throwing a baseball 252 feet, 4½ inches.

The Baseball Slaughter of 1950

NEVER BEFORE IN THE HISTORY OF MAJOR LEAGUE baseball have so many runs been rolled up by one team in a single game as in the slugfest between the Boston Red Sox and the St. Louis Browns at Fenway Park on June 8, 1950. It started in the second inning with 8 runs and by the time the fifth inning died down the score was 22 to 3 in favor of Boston. When it was all over, the score stood 29 to 4 and the scoreboard looked like this:

										R	H	E
St. Louis	0	0	3	0	0	0	0	0	1	4	6	1
Boston	0	8	5	7	2	0	2	5	x	29	28	0

Now this was all the more fantastic when one considers that the previous day brought this same Boston team 20 runs in their atomic blasting of the same St. Louis team, and the total number of runs for two consecutive games beat all previous records in major league baseball history with 49 runs.

But that is not all. Other records were broken. The Red Sox scored the most total bases (60) in any single game ever played in the major leagues. Williams (lf), Dropo (1b) and Doerr (2b) made a nice trio hitting 7 home runs among them and almost tying the all-time record of 8 homers hit in any single game.

Unfortunately for the Red Sox and fortunately for the Browns, there were only 5,105 fans present to see the massacre.

A Seventy-Game Set of Tennis

AT THE HEART OF AMERICA TOURNAMENT IN KANSAS City in the summer of 1968, two players named Brown—tall Bill of Omaha, Nebraska, and short John of Melbourne, Australia—played the longest recorded set of singles in tennis history. It lasted nearly three hours and when it was over, John beat Bill, 36-34. It was the first set of a best-of-three-sets match, and John was so fortified by finally outlasting his opponent in the marathon set that he closed out the match with an easy 6-1 victory in the second set.

The longest singles match in history was played in Warsaw, Poland, in 1966, between England's Roger Taylor and Wieslaw Gasiorek of Poland. Taylor finally prevailed, 29-27, 31-29, 6-4, after 126 games. The match was part of the King's Cup indoor tournament, between several European nations. Amazingly, Taylor engaged in another long struggle with another Polish player, Taddeus Nowicki, in the same tournament. Their first set, which Taylor won, 33-31, was the third longest ever recorded, and the Englishman went on to a 6-1 victory in the second set.

For marathon tennis, however, one has to look at doubles competition, which places such a high premium on keeping balls in play. In the second round of the Newport (R.I.) Casino Tournament in 1967, Dick Leach of Arcadia, California, and Dick Dell of Bethesda, Maryland, were teamed against Len Schloss of Baltimore and Tom Mozur of Sweetwater, Tennessee. The first set went routinely to Schloss and Mozur, 6-3. But by the time the final ball was struck, the players had struggled through 147 games, the longest match of any kind on record, including an unbelievable second set won by Leach and Dell, 49-47. The Leach-Dell duo also won the third and deciding set, 22-20.

One Man, Two Highest Point Totals

CLARENCE (BEVO) FRANCIS, A 6-9 CENTER, BECAME almost a legend during his collegiate basketball career at Rio Grande College in Ohio during the early 1950's. And with good reason. During his two years of devastation, the Hammondsville, Ohio, sensation averaged 50.1 points per game in 1952-53 and "slumped" to 47.1 points per game in 1953-54. In 68 games with Bevo, Rio Grande won 61. His two most sensational scoring outbursts still stand as the greatest single scoring nights in the game's history and may never be broken. During the 1952-53 season he drilled in 47 baskets and 22 free throws for *116 points* as Rio Grande lashed Ashland Junior College of Kentucky, 150-85. The next season Bevo bombed the nets for 38 baskets and 37 free throws for *113 points* in a 134-91 Rio Grande victory over Hillsdale College of Michigan.

Speed in Sports

THE ELEMENT OF SPEED PLAYS A LARGE PART IN many sports, but it can be best illustrated by listing several of the major sporting records involving speed:

On October 23, 1970, Gary Gabelich drove his jet-powered "Blue Flame" through the measured mile at the Bonneville Salt Flats in Utah at a new land record speed of 622.407 miles per hour.

On August 24, 1968, Dr. Fager, a four-year-old colt, raced a mile in one minute, 32 1/5 seconds at Arlington Park in Chicago, the fastest mile clocking ever posted by a horse.

Jim Ryun, the great mile runner from Kansas, gave the greatest performance of his career at Bakersfield, California, on June 23, 1967, covering the mile in a world record time of three minutes, 51.1 seconds.

The Most Dramatic Moment in Sports

WHEN THE ASSOCIATED PRESS ATTEMPTED TO DEtermine in 1950 which was sport's most dramatic moment of the twentieth century, they were just one year too soon. Bobby Thomson struck a blow for the New York Giants against the Brooklyn Dodgers on October 3, 1951, that brought the Giants the National League pennant in one swing, and has become known as "the shot heard around the world," because the critical game was broadcast around the world that day.

Here are the most drama-laden moments in all of sports history:

Bobby Thomson's home run gives Giants pennant, 1951.
Don Larsen pitches perfect game in World Series, 1956.
Baltimore Colts win NFL title from New York Giants in "sudden death" overtime, 1958.
Bob Beamon long jumps 29-2½ at Mexico City Olympics, 1958.

BOBBY THOMSON'S HOME RUN: On August 12, 1951, the Brooklyn Dodgers seemed to have the National League pennant race well in hand. They led the second-place New York Giants by a seemingly insurmountable 13½ games. But the Giants won 37 of their last 44 games and the Dodgers slumped, and the teams closed out the regular season in a tie. A three-game playoff was scheduled, and the Giants won the first game, the Dodgers the second. Then, on October 3, at the Polo Grounds, the whole season was reduced to one day. The Dodgers breezed into the ninth inning leading 4-1 and looked as safe as they had on August 12 with that 13½ game lead. Then the Giants put together two singles and a double for a run, causing Brooklyn manager Chuck Dressen to replace Don Newcombe, his starting pitcher, with Ralph Branca. With Thomson, a dangerous hitter scheduled to bat and first base open, the strategy seemed to dictate an intentional walk. The next scheduled batter was a slumping rookie centerfielder named Willie Mays. But Dressen ordered Branca to pitch to Thomson. The first delivery, with Giant runners dancing off second and third, was a low fast ball that Thomson took for a strike. The next pitch was a high fast ball that Thomson seemed to be expecting and he ripped it deep to left field on a line. It was a sure hit, but would it clear the wall? It did, and the Polo Grounds and Giant fans everywhere went berserk. The New Yorkers had won the National League pennant, 5-4.

The 1950 voting produced these results in the AP poll:

318 SPORTS EXPERTS VOTING

1. The Dempsey-Firpo fight of 1923	*70 votes*
2. Babe Ruth "calling his home run," 1932	*66 votes*
3. Dempsey-Tunney "long count" fight, 1927	*43 votes*
4. Lou Gehrig's farewell, 1939	*23 votes*

DEMPSEY-FIRPO FIGHT: Took place at the Polo Grounds in New York on September 14, 1923. Dempsey, the World's Heavyweight Champion, was considered the greatest fighter of all and Luis Firpo, the "Wild Bull of the Pampas," was a tough challenger. The fight lasted 3 minutes and 7 seconds and was witnessed by a wild hysterical crowd of 82,000. Dempsey knocked Firpo down nine times in this short and furious fight and Firpo knocked Dempsey down twice. Toward the end of round one, after being knocked down six times, Firpo sent a hard right to Dempsey's jaw and knocked him out of the ropes and into the laps of newsmen. The shock of seeing the heavyweight king sprawled out and apparently helpless will never be forgotten by those who witnessed it. Dempsey, dazed, groggy and badly hurt, got back into the ring at the count of 9 and Firpo had the chance of his life but missed it. One good blow would have put Dempsey to sleep, but that blow did not come. In the second round Dempsey finished off Firpo and kept the heavyweight title. Thus ended the most furious and exciting fight in heavyweight history.

MISCELLANEOUS

Conquering the Northwest Passage

ONE OF THE MOST ADVENTUROUS VOYAGES OF THE 1960's did not occur in space, but in an unpassable stretch of Arctic sea from Canada to Alaska. The journey of the *S.S. Manhattan* succeeded in conquering the fabled Northwest Passage, a goal of North American explorers since Lewis and Clark. This journey was a remarkable achievement of modern technology, and of the pioneering spirit of the *Manhattan's* crew. The ship ploughed through vast wastes of Arctic ice, its men were exposed to lashing winds and inhuman cold. At one point the whole venture appeared doomed. It seemed that the ship must turn back; against all odds captain and crew decided to go on, while the world watched their struggle and their victory.

The ship that forged an Arctic sea path from Canada to Alaska is the most powerful icebreaker ever built. It has a unique 125-foot bow that moves the vessel up and over the ice in a slow-motion chopping movement, breaking the ice with the weight of the ship. It is protected against the tremendous pressure of the ice by steel belts along the hull, and it carries two helicopters on its landing deck. Owned by the Humble Oil & Refining Co., the *S.S. Manhattan* will bring oil from Alaska to the East Coast via the newly opened Northwest Passage.

The Biggest Blackout

AT 5:27 P.M. ON NOVEMBER 9, 1965, THE LIGHTS in New York City went out. Elevators stalled, subways stopped, televisions went blank. The country's largest metropolitan area was trapped in sudden darkness and immobility. It was the beginning of the greatest power failure in history, extending 80,000 square miles across northeastern United States and Canada. It affected 30,000,000 people—hospitals switched to their own generators, the only news came from transistor radios, and transportation networks were clogged with non-moving vehicles. Power was gradually restored throughout various areas, and by the evening of November 10, all the lights were on again. The world's biggest blackout was over.

The Largest Statue in the World

THE STATUE OF LIBERTY IN NEW YORK HARBOR IS so well known and information about it is so easily obtained from encyclopedias and almanacs that it seems hardly necessary to describe it here. What is *not* so well known about it is that it actually is the largest statute in the world today; yet no description of it mentions this fact. It was designed by the Alsatian sculptor Fredrick Augustus Bartholdi, whose mother, Charlotte Beysser Bartholdi, was the model. The original statue was 9 feet high and was enlarged to 32 feet. From this miniature the final large figure was calculated by the famous Gustave Eiffel, designer of the Eiffel Tower. The statue was begun in 1874 and finished in 1883. It was formally presented to the United States by France on July 4, 1884. Here are a few of the dimensions:

From the base of the statue to the tip of the torch is 151 feet, 1 inch.
From the base of the pedestal to the tip of the torch is 305 feet, 6 inches.
Length of the right arm is 42 feet.
Length of the hand is 16 feet, 5 inches.
Length of the index finger is 8 feet.
Size of the fingernail is 13 inches by 10 inches.
Thickness of the waist is 35 feet.

The statue weighs 450,000 pounds and its total cost was between $500,000 and $600,000.

The Largest Corporation in the World

THE LARGEST CORPORATION IS NOT THE STANDARD Oil Company or the United States Steel Corporation, nor is it the Metropolitan Life Insurance Company.

The winner and champion is the American Telephone and Telegraph Company with total assets of more than $34,123,000,000, as of January 1, 1970. A huge tax amounts to a tax of more than $2.00 a month for every one of the 80,000,000 telephones that are now inter-connected throughout the United States.

No other corporation in the world has the enormous assets of the American Tel and Tel and no other corporation can boast of more than 3,000,000 stockholders.

The Priceless Morse or Cope Button

MOST PEOPLE NEVER THINK OF BUTTONS AS BEING particularly valuable. Buttons are something to be sewed on clothing, and their serviceability is nearly always far greater than their intrinsic value.

But just as there are stamp collectors so there are button collectors, and just as there are stamps of enormous value so there are buttons of enormous value.

The most valuable and rarest button in the world is in Rome. It is a magnificent work of art executed by Benvenuto Cellini in 1530 especially for Pope Clement who described it as "a piece of the very greatest consequence."

The button, known as the "Morse" or "Cope" button, is large, round and flat, measuring six inches in diameter. It is made of gold and decorated with a beautiful diamond together with other gems of the greatest value. The design shows God, the Father, in half relief directly over the central diamond. According to the dates given by Cellini it required a year and a half to complete the button and, in addition to his own priceless skill, he employed a staff of ten craftsmen to help him out. The drawing is made from a reproduction in the November, 1949, issue of *The National Button Bulletin*. The design is described by the master as follows:

> I had put the diamond exactly in the centre of the piece and above it God, the Father, was shown seated, leaning nobly in a sideways attitude, which made a perfect composition, and did not interfere with the stone's effect. Lifting His right hand He was in the act of giving the benediction. Below the diamond I had placed three children, who, with their arms upraised, were supporting the jewel. All around I set a crowd of cherubs in divers attitudes, adapted to the other gems. A mantle undulated to the wind around the figure of the Father, from which cherubs peeped out; and there were other ornaments besides which made a very beautiful effect.

According to the authorities in the National Button Society this is the rarest and the most beautiful button in the world.

Ice Water in all the Rooms

THE AALESUND IS A RED WOODEN BUILDING ERECTED by a Norwegian Coal Company in Spitzbergen. It is the world's most northerly hotel, being only 650 miles from the North Pole.

Tiny Drawbridge

SOMERSET BRIDGE AT ELY'S HARBOR IN BERMUDA IS the smallest drawbridge. The two draws open up and allow only one sailboat to pass through at a time. The length of each draw is actually less than its width and the total length of the bridge is under 20 feet.

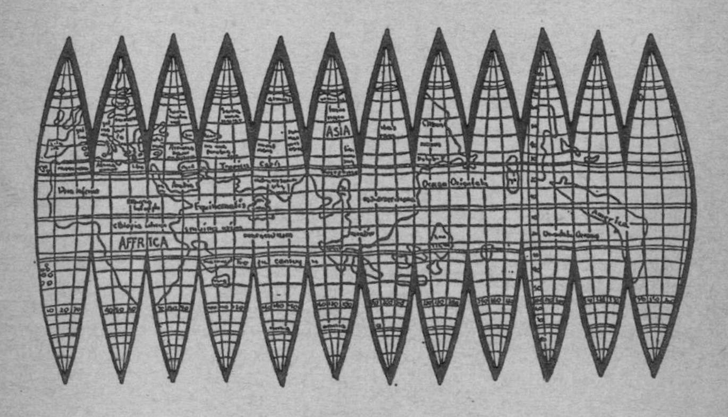

$50,000 for One Map

UNDOUBTEDLY THE MOST VALUABLE MAP IN THE world and certainly the rarest was shown on May 24, 1950, at the Parke-Bernet Galleries in New York City.

The title of the Parke-Bernet Galleries catalogue reads as follows: "The World Renowned *Hauslab-Liechtenstein* World Global Map of 1507 by Matin Waldseemüller. The only known copy of the first published globular map of the Western Hemisphere and the first globular map on which the name *America* appears."

The owner of this valuable map, who did not give his name, refused an offer of $50,000 for it and stated that he would offer it for sale at auction May 24, but would refuse all bids unless they exceeded $50,000.

The map is described as a priceless Xylographic Print and the only one in existence printed from a single wood block neither reworked nor disfigured by coloring. It is in perfect condition and measures 15 inches in length and 9½ inches in height. It is credited as being the first map to suggest that the newly discovered continent be called *America* after the explorer

Amerigo Vespucci. Note the name *America* on the three right-hand segments.

The map went back to its owner after the auction sale as nobody offered more than $50,000 for it.

32,284,980 Strikes and Still Going Strong

TO THE RIGHT OF THE PORTAL IN THE FAMOUS CAthedral of Notre Dame in Dijon, France, is the oldest going clock in the world. Made by Jacques Marc and presented to the town in 1383 by Philip the Hardy, this clock has been keeping excellent time ever since. Two large bronze figures shown here strike the hour every hour and have been doing this for 567 years. Up to January 1, 1950, the number of times these figures have struck was 32,284,980. Jacquemart, as the clock is called, is one of the main sights in Dijon.

The Words Champion

ACCORDING TO THE WORLD ALMANAC FOR 1950, Frank R. Fraprie, after counting more than 240,000 words from fifteen authors and many magazines and newspapers, found the most commonly used English words to be in the following order:

1. the	4. to	7. that	10. it
2. of	5. a	8. is	11. for
3. and	6. in	9. I	12. as

Anyone who wants to verify this need only count the number of *the's* on any page of any book or magazine or newspaper and compare this number with the number of other words like *and* and *for*. The word most frequently used in everyday conversation is *I*, proving that we are all more or less egoists.

THE MOST USED LETTER IN ENGLISH

Everyone knows that the small letter e is used more than any other but few know the order of use of the next ten. This is:

t, a, i, s, o, n, h, r, d, u

The letter that begins most of the English words is *s*, which begins about 37,000 words. According to the Merriam-Webster dictionary, the approximate number of words for the next ten initial letters is:

c	29,000	m	15,000
p	28,000	d	14,400
a	19,700	r	14,200
t	17,200	f	11,800
b	15,000	h	11,200

If you look through that dictionary you'll see why *s* is the "champion" initial letter. You'll be surprised to find that every consonant except b and x combines with s, and you'll find such words as:

sdrucciola sforzando sganarelle sjambok
sruti ssu svarga

No other letter in the dictionary has as many combining letters as *s*.

The Largest English Word

IT IS NOT AN EASY MATTER TO DETERMINE THE longest word in the English language. Words of 23 and 24 letters are fairly common and it is only when we get into the 30's that we begin to approach word giants. Many people claim the famous *antidisestablishmentarianism* as the longest but that has only 26 letters and becomes a sort of abbreviation next to *semiphotospectroheliographically* or *antiinterdenominationalistically* each of which has 32 letters. While these are genuine words with many prefixes and suffixes they are not in the dictionary.

Of course, there are chemical names that are nothing more than many combinations of groups like the phenol group or the amino group, but these hardly could be called English words. Here are three of them just for practice:

tetraazodiaminotriphenolmethane
hydroxiquinoldibenzolmetholacitol
paraoxymentametboxyallybenzene

and, of course

paraminobenzoyldiaethylaminoaethanolumphydrochloricum.

Half an Acre of Flag

THE AVERAGE AMERICAN FLAG THAT IS DISPLAYED on national holidays is 4 feet wide and 7 feet long. In comparing an average flag to the largest flag in the world, the *length* of the average American flag is just the *width of one of the stripes* in the giant flag. This colossal banner is 270 feet long and 90 feet wide and covers slightly more than half an acre of ground. The blue union is large enough to cover a tennis court and each star is as tall as the average woman. As the thirteen stripes are each 7 feet wide the flag is broad enough for a dozen automobiles to drive along it 12 abreast; the 24,300 square feet of bunting in the flag weigh 1,048 pounds. In the 45 days it took to make it, 90 workers used up 13½ miles of thread in sewing 952 yards of red strips, 849 yards of white strips and 260 yards of blue strips together.

This flag was made by Annin & Company of New York for the J. L. Hudson Company in Detroit. The original flag was 90 feet wide by 150 feet long and was first displayed on November 11, 1922, outside Hudson's store as shown in this picture. A few years later Annin & Company added another 120 feet and the flag was displayed at the New York World's Fair in 1939. It is now the property of J. L. Hudson Company.

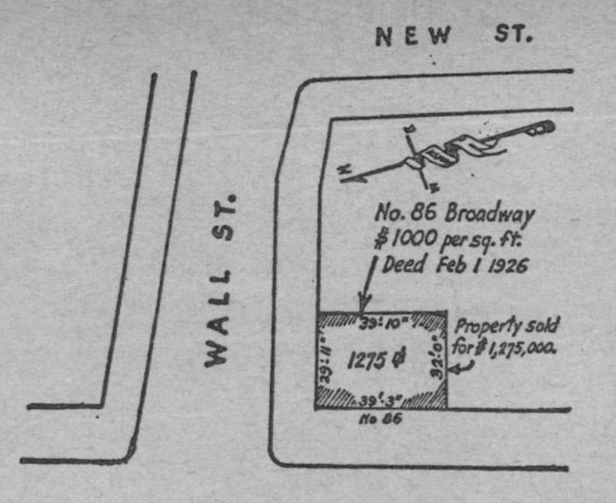

A Plot that Sold for $7.00 per Square Inch

LAND IS USUALLY SOLD BY THE ACRE, AND AN ACRE is 43,560 square feet. In our large cities property is sold in lots and the average lot is 25 feet by 100 feet. Of course the price that the lot will bring depends upon its location.

According to a deed dated and recorded February 1, 1926, the 265 Fourth Avenue Corporation sold to the 1 Wall Street Realty Corporation at 80 Broadway, New York City, a piece of property on the corner of Broadway and Wall Street in New York. The price paid for this property was $1,275,000 and the total area of the plot was only 1,275 square feet. This price of $1,000 per square foot for land is, as far as is known, the highest ever paid anywhere in the world. According to real estate authorities it tops everything in real estate values and has never been equaled. On this site there was an 18-story office building valued at $200,000 but that was many years ago. There were also other plots in the immediate vicinity selling for enormous sums, but today they are all combined into one huge parcel of land and occupied by the Irving Trust Company.

Incidentally, $1,000 per square foot amounts to $43,560,000 per acre.

High Life with Father

IN SPITE OF ALL THE BRILLIANT SUCCESSES MORE recently on Broadway such as *South Pacific, Hello Dolly* and others, *Life with Father* is still the play that had the longest run—3223 performances. The total gross income from this remarkable run amounted to between 8½ and 9 million dollars and the backers were paid $60 for every dollar they invested. The play was produced by Oscar Serlin.

At one time there were three *Life with Father* companies all playing at once, two on the road and one in New York. As the months rolled by and turned into years the children naturally outgrew their parts, so every six or eight months a new set of four red-headed youngsters had to be selected to play the parts of father's four children.

The largest and most amazing moving picture contract on record was the leasing of *Life with Father* to Warner Brothers for a period of seven years. The contract stipulated that after that time all rights reverted back to the owners, Howard Lindsay, Russel Crouse and Mrs. Clarence Day. Warner Brothers paid $500,000 down on the contract against the following percentage:

1. 28½ per cent of the gross to be paid to the owners until the picture has paid for itself.
2. 41 per cent of the gross to be paid to the owners after the picture has paid for itself.

As far as we know there has never been any play or movie contract that carried with it such phenomenal success. The nearest competitor was *Tobacco Road* with 3,182 performances and *Abie's Irish Rose* with 2,327.

The City in the Clouds

THE HIGHEST CITY IN THE WORLD IS LA PAZ, THE capital of Bolivia. Located 11,900 feet (more than two miles) above sea level, the air is rare and the temperatures are low through the year in spite of the fact that La Paz is in the tropics. The streets of La Paz are steep and very irregular and the surrounding mountains rise 1,500 feet above the city to the margin of the great Lake Titicaca plateau. The 1942 population of the city was 287,029. Incidentally, those who think Lhasa, in Tibet, is the world's highest city, are wrong by 70 feet. The elevation of Lhasa is 11,830 feet.

The Greatest Density of Population

ACCORDING TO RECENT STATISTICS THE MOST densely populated territory in the world is the Province of Macao on the southern coast of China. Its small area of 6.2 square miles had a population in 1965 of 280,000 which is a density of 45,000 people per square mile.

The World's Most Valuable Stamp

THE ORIGINAL OF THE STRANGE-LOOKING OBJECT shown here is colored magenta. If you saw it lying on the sidewalk, it is a safe bet you would pass it by or, if you did happen to pick it up, you would probably throw it away thinking it was a revenue stamp on some foreign brand of cigarette package.

If, however, you are a philatelist, you would snatch it up as fast as you could. It is a reproduction of the rarest and most valuable stamp in the world, the one-cent magenta of British Guiana of 1856, and its present owner has refused $60,000 for it. No other copies of this rare stamp have ever come to light in spite of intense search, so stamp collectors offer all kinds of fancy prices for it.

The stamp has an interesting history. In 1855, because of delay in deliveries, the supply of stamps in British Guiana was exhausted and the postmaster ordered a new issue from the printing office. The design was the same as the issue of 1853 and, to prevent forgery, the stamp was initialed by the postal clerk before sale. The stamps were quickly used up and they soon went out of circulation.

This "most valuable stamp in the world" was discovered in 1873 and was sold to N. R. McKinnon for 6 shillings. Five years later a dealer in Liverpool bought it for 110 pounds (about $500 at that time). In 1922, at a Paris auction sale, this stamp was sold to a Mr. Arthur Hind for $37,000, the highest price ever paid for a single stamp up to that time.

When Arthur Hind died the stamp became the property of his widow, who on August 7, 1940 sold it to Finbar Kenny, manager of Macy's Philatelic Center for $45,000. Mr. Kenny bought the stamp for a collector who wishes to remain anonymous and who has recently refused an offer of $60,000 for it.

The Most Expensive Painting Ever Auctioned

IN DECEMBER OF 1970, A PORTRAIT BY DIEGO Velásquez came up for sale at a London auction. It was all over in two minutes and another world record had been made. The painting sold for five million, five hundred, forty-four thousand dollars ($5,544,000), making it the highest priced work of art ever sold at auction, more than doubling the previous record for a Rembrandt nine years earlier.

The portrait of Velásquez' painting assistant, Juan de Pareja, is considered the finest work of this seventeenth century Spanish master. It aroused tremendous acclaim when it was painted in 1649, with its overpowering, commanding presence, and it won Velásquez election to the Academy of St. Luke. Its present owners are the international art firm of Wildenstein & Company, which bought it from the Earl of Radnor.

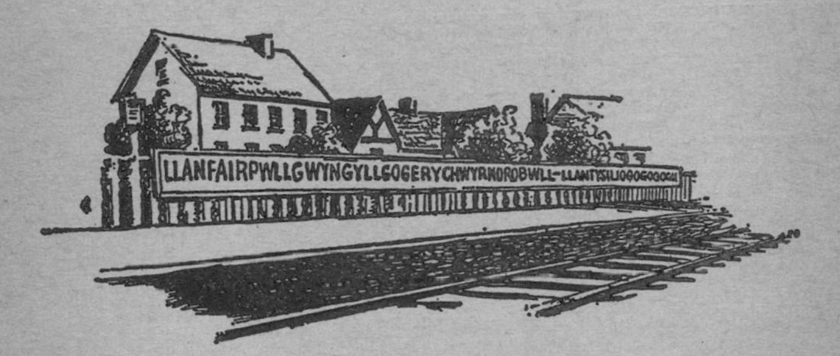

A Name as Long as a Train

THERE IS A LITTLE TOWN ON THE ISLAND OF Anglesey in North Wales just about a mile from the famous Britannia Bridge. The town is noted for its many quarries of building stone but its chief claim to fame lies in its extraordinary name which is

Llanfairpwllgwyngyllgogerychwyrndrobwll-Llantysiliogogogoch.

This 58-letter mouthful translated into English means

"The church place of Saint Mary by the pool of the White Hazel by the rapid whirlpool of the Church of Saint Silligog of the Red Cave."

Now, of course, the conductor on the train does not say: "next stop Llanfairpwllgwyngyllgogerychwyrndrobwll-Llantysiliogogogoch" nor does he give the English translation. He merely shouts out "Llanfair next" (pronounced Pflanfair) and lets it go at that.

As far as we are able to determine, this full name is the longest of any city or town in the world. The drawing was taken from a photograph of the Llanfair station. The sign bearing the name is almost as long as the average train that pulls into the station. Don't look for this big name on the map—it isn't there.

The World's Oldest Murder Trial

THE VERY FIRST RECORD OF A MURDER TRIAL DATES back nearly 4,000 years. In March, 1950, a number of archeologists from the Universities of Chicago and Pennsylvania reported that they had unearthed a small tablet which describes how three men killed another man and then informed his wife, who failed to notify the authorities. The case, however, became known and was brought before King Ur-Ninurta, who turned it over for a trial to the citizens' committee of Nippur. In this assembly nine men started to prosecute the three murderers as well as the wife of the murdered man but, after much argument, two men got up and spoke in the wife's defense saying that she had nothing to do with the crime. They argued that since her husband did not support her she had a right to remain silent about the murder. Apparently this had its effect because the woman was set free and the three murderers were executed.

This interesting story of antiquity was written on a two-by-four-inch clay tablet found in Iraq about 100 miles south of Bagdad. It took place in 1850 B.C. The story was written in cuneiform script in the Sumerian language and was translated by doctors Samuel Noah Kramer and Thorkild Jacobsen. It is the oldest known record of a murder trial and reveals that in those early times they used the same basic law that we use today.

1 Metropolitan Life Insurance Company

WARRANT NUMBER 124250 DETAIL $225,000,000.00 PRINCIPAL AMOUNT OF UNITED STATES OF AMERICA, 2 1/2 % TREASURY BONDS, DATED APRIL 15,1943, DUE JUNE 15, 1959.

PAY TO THE ORDER OF THE CHASE NATIONAL BANK OF THE CITY OF NEW YORK $225,000,000.00

EXACTLY $225,000,000 AND 00/100 DOLLARS

To The Chase National Bank of the City of New York Metropolitan Branch

The Largest Check

THE LARGEST CHECK ISSUED SO FAR IN THE WORLD was paid January 1, 1961, by the Continental Illinois National Bank & Trust Company of Chicago. The check was made out to Sears Roebuck & Company in the amount of $960,242,000,000.

The Smallest Country

UNTIL FEBRUARY, 1929, THE TINY PRINCIPALITY OF Monaco, with a population of only 21,000 and an area a little more than half a square mile, was the smallest country in the world. On February 11, 1929, however, the Lateran Agreement between Cardinal Gasparri and Mussolini was signed and Vatican City, now an independent state with its own police force, its own stamps and its own money, became the smallest country.

Imagine, if you can, an independent country not a quarter the size of Central Park in New York City and you'll have some idea of the size of the Vatican City State—a country so small that you could walk across it in fifteen minutes—with a railway, a newspaper and an independent broadcasting station. This miniature, the smallest country in the world, has diplomatic relations with 42 countries.

On the 108.7 acres (0.16 square mile) of Vatican City State are located St. Peter's, the Vatican Palace and museum and the Vatican gardens. There are thirteen buildings which house the officers necessary for the administration of the church. Police duties are carried out by Pontifican Arms Corps, which comprise the

Swiss Guards, the Noble Guards and the Palatine Guards of Honor and the Pontifical Gendarmerie. A tiny railroad, the shortest in the world, makes its complete run of six-tenths of a mile in a little more than a minute and serves the entire population of 1,025 (about one-sixth the seating capacity of the Radio City Music Hall in New York).

When Vatican City became Vatican City State in 1929 the usual street cleaning force appeared to clean its streets but, because nobody was allowed in the state without credentials, the force was shut out for days and the tiny state's streets had to go dirty. This condition became so acute that the Governor had to admit the street cleaners from Rome, and today the Vatican City State is the only independent country in the world to employ "foreign help" to clean its streets.

The legal system is based on the canon law. The pope has full legal, executive and judicial powers. Executivc power over Vatican City State is given over to the governor who is responsible to the pope.

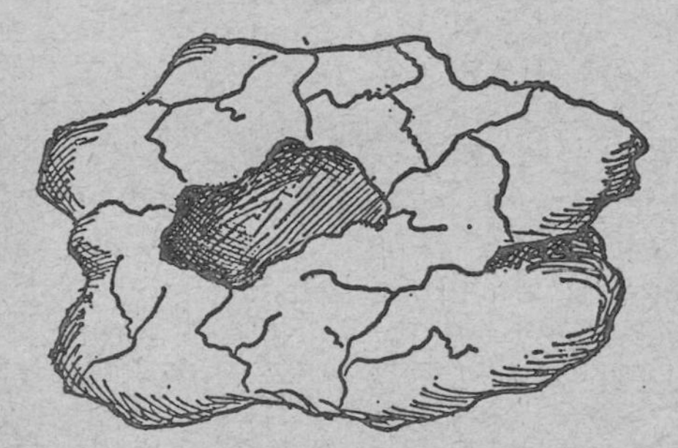

The Oldest Piece of Food in the World

IN A MUSEUM IN CAIRO, EGYPT, THERE IS WHAT REmains of a loaf of bread that was found in the tomb of one of the ancient Egyptian queens. This loaf is claimed to be between 4,000 and 5,000 years old.

Long Name Lake

MOST PEOPLE HAVE HEARD OF LONG LAKE IN NORTHern New York State but few have ever heard of the lake with the longest name. It is near Webster, Massachusetts, only three miles from the Connecticut state line on state route 193. This is a 14-syllable name, with 40 letters in it, which is Indian in origin. It is:

Lake Chargogagogmanchaugagogchaubunagungamaug

which translated into English means: "You fish on your side, we fish on our side, nobody fish in the middle."

It is known locally as Lake Webster.

The World's Largest Clocks

SEVERAL YEARS AGO A CLOCK WITH A DIAL MADE OF cement was installed on the ground of the airport of Durban, South Africa. The dimensions of this huge clock are 200 feet in diameter, with a minute hand slightly more than 95 feet long and the spaces between the minute marks over 10 feet. The hands are driven electrically and the tip of the minute hand travels 2½ inches every second or about 6 miles per day. Airplanes can see this great timepiece for miles around.

For years the great clock atop the Colgate Building in Jersey City, New Jersey, was the largest in the world. It is still the largest vertical clock today. The dial is 50 feet in diameter with an area of 1,963 square feet. The hands are made of seven-ply wood tapered from the hub to the tip. The minute hand measures 27 feet 3 inches long exclusive of the length of the counterbalance which is 10 feet. The hand is 20 inches thick and weighs a little more than a ton. The hour hand is 19½ feet long and 18 inches thick, weighing 1,725 pounds. The tip of the minute hand travels 155 feet per hour or three-quarters of a mile every day. The clock has a pendulum 8 feet long carrying a weight of 230 pounds. Power is furnished to the motors, which operate the clock by twenty-eight large-volt batteries which are automatically recharged. The clock can run for four days without recharging the batteries.

The Tallest Structure

THE TALLEST STRUCTURE IN THE WORLD IS NOT THE new World Trade Center in New York, as you might imagine. It happens to be in North Dakota. It is a TV transmitting tower 2,063 feet high (713 feet higher than the World Trade Center) located between Fargo and Blanchard, North Dakota at a cost of $5,000,000. It is owned by the Pembine Broadcasting Company of North Dakota and represents Channel 11 of KTHI-TV. This amazing transmitting tower has a cage elevator in the center rising 1,948 feet.

The Largest Painting Ever Executed by Man

JOHN BANVARD WAS BORN IN NEW YORK CITY ON November 15, 1815. Because of financial reverses in his family he had to leave school and make his own way in the world at the age of fifteen. His first job was that of a drug clerk in Louisville, Kentucky, but he wasted so much time making sketches and not attending to customers that he was soon fired.

Banvard shifted from job to job until, at the age of twenty-five, he suddenly made up his mind that he would paint a panorama of the Mississippi River from its source to the city of New Orleans. Now with most young men this would be just a wild dream since such an undertaking is almost beyond human endeavor, but Banvard was not like most young men. He worked at odd jobs and saved enough money to buy a tiny skiff and start out on the venture. For more than 400 days and nights he lived on the banks of the river, hunting his food by day and sleeping under his skiff at night. Many a stormy night was spent sitting on a log to escape any caving in of the banks of the river or possibly a falling tree.

How many sketches Banvard made is not known—perhaps thousands. All of them were carefully drawn and accurately represented the entire length of the Mississippi. When he finished this enormous task he was penniless so he went to work again to earn enough to build himself a makeshift studio outside of Louisville and, from the cotton mills in Lowell, Massachusetts, to buy more than *three miles* of canvas on which to paint some 1,200 miles of panorama—"the largest painting ever executed by man."

Banvard's friend, Selium Woodworth, describes his work in the following letter:

> . . . Banvard immediately conducted us into the interior of the building . . . Within the studio all seemed chaos and confusion but the life-like and natural appearance of a portion of his great picture, displayed on one of the walls in a yet unfinished state. Here and there were scattered about the floor piles of his original sketches, bales of canvas and heaps of boxes. Paint-pots, brushes, jars and kegs were strewed about without order or arrangement while along one of the walls several large cases were piled containing rolls of finished sections of the painting.
>
> On the opposite wall was spread a canvas extending its whole length upon which the artist was at work. A

> portion of the canvas was wound upon an upright roller, or drum, standing at one end of the building and, as the artist completes his painting he thus disposes of it. Not having time to spare I could not stay to have all the immense cylinders unrolled for our inspection. . . . Any description of this gigantic undertaking that I should attempt in a letter would convey but a faint idea of what it will be when completed. The remarkable truthfulness of the minutest objects upon the shores of the river, independent of the masterly style and artistical execution of the work, will make it the most valuable historical painting in the world and unequaled for magnitude and variety of interest by any work that has ever been heard of since the art of painting was discovered.

Banvard first exhibited his remarkable painting in Louisville—three miles of canvas wound around drums and slowly unfolding for two hours before the eyes of the observer. The first showing was a total failure but soon enough people heard about it and before long the people flocked to see Banvard's Panorama. From then on Banvard was a made man. In 1846 he took his panorama to Boston and the following year to New York. In 1848 he went abroad and showed it in Manchester, Liverpool, Bath and London. He died an extremely wealthy man on May 16, 1891.

In full justice to fact it must be noted that Banvard's Panorama was definitely *not* a work of art. Banvard was entirely untutored and this work's value was chiefly geographical without artistic merit or technical skill. It is no longer in existence and, as far as is known, no photographs were ever made of it. The last that was heard of it was that parts of it were cut up to make backdrops in some local theaters in Watertown, South Dakota. It is also doubtful that the painting was three miles long—more likely it was not more than a mile. But it is the largest painting known to be executed by man.

The illustration is based on a picture in the Missouri Historical Society.

The Most Valuable Theatrical Property

THE MOST PROFITABLE PROPERTIES EVER CREATED in the entire history of the theatre in any period or time or in any language are the operas of Gilbert and Sullivan. In addition, the collaboration between Gilbert and Sullivan was the greatest in history and 11 of the 14 operas which they produced will live forever. The best known of the Gilbert and Sullivan works are *Pinafore, Mikado* and *The Pirates of Penzance, Iolanthe* and *Yeoman of the Guard.* In the late 1870s there were as many as 100 different companies playing *Pinafore* in America all at the same time; eight of them were in New York. By 1950 the D'Oyly Carte Opera Company had given more than 25,000 performances of the various operas which, in terms of cash, runs into the millions. In addition to the D'Oyly Carte productions in England there had been thousands of productions in this country so that the grand total of all Gilbert and Sullivan operas produced since 1875 was well above sixty thousand.

The World's Longest Pipeline

A NATURAL GAS PIPELINE EXTENDING FROM BROWNSville, Texas, to 134th Street and the Hudson River in New York was opened on January 16, 1951. This line is the longest pipeline in the world and represents one of the most remarkable engineering problems in history. It is 1,832 miles long and crosses 40 rivers. It has 476 miles of connecting pipeline and 19 compressor stations at an average of 80 miles apart, to boost and maintain pressure along the line. The line brings natural gas from the Texas wells to the "front door" of New York City, although the gas takes four days to make the trip. The line was built by the Fish Engineering Corporation of Houston in only twenty months.

The Smallest Piece of Real Estate in the World

UP TO A FEW YEARS AGO (1947) THERE WAS A little triangular corner on Seventh Avenue and Christopher in New York that was isolated through a surveying error. It was called the "Property of the Hess Estate" and the total area of the land came to 308 square inches. The triangle was 26″ x 27″ x 27″, just about four times as long as this book, and taxes of $3.00 a year were paid by the estate. This amazing piece of property in America's largest city was just large enough to stand on, but of course it would be impossible to walk on it because a step in any direction would take you off it. It was recently merged with the adjoining property.

INDEX